Walking the Coastline
of Shetland

No. 6

South Mainland

"Oft at evening I've wandered
By the shore, in pensive mood.
Finding there a deeper meaning,
A true charm in solitude.
And my heart, alone with Nature,
Marked the murmur of the sea
With an agony of longing
Conscious of its mystery".

James J. Haldane Burgess

J. J. Haldane Burgess (1862-1927) was a Shetland scholar, poet and writer of novels and Shetland verse. He gradually became blind whilst studying at Edinburgh University but his creativity remained undiminished. He is chiefly remembered today for "Rasmies' Buddie" and the words of "The Up Helly Aa Song" written in 1897 and set to music by Dr T. M. Y. Manson. Both were Lerwick men.

Walking the Coastline of Shetland

No. 6

South Mainland

Peter Guy

The coastline of South Mainland,
circular walks and the islands of
St. Ninian's
South Havra
Mousa
Trondra
West Burra
East Burra
Fair Isle

Published by
The Shetland Times Ltd.,
Lerwick, Shetland.
2000

Walking the Coastline of Shetland – South Mainland.

ISBN 978 1 898852 64 3

First published by The Shetland Times Ltd., 2000.
Reprinted 2008.

A CIP catalogue record for this book is available from the British Library.

Books in the same series

No. 1 The Island of Yell
No. 2 The Island of Unst
No. 3 The Island of Fetlar
No. 4 Northmavine
No. 5 Westside
No. 6 South Mainland
No. 7 Eastside

Cover Photographs:

Front cover – main picture: Mousa Broch © Colin Wilson
Inserts: Sumburgh Lighthouse © Hugh Harrop
White-sided dolphins © Hugh Harrop

Back cover: Whale watcher © Hugh Harrop

Printed and published by
The Shetland Times Ltd., Gremista, Lerwick,
Shetland ZE1 0PX, Scotland.

Dr Mortimer Manson accompanies the Yell bairns at the Market Cross, Lerwick.　　　　　John Coutts

Dedicated to the memory of Dr T M Y Manson (1904-1996) of Lerwick.
A writer and musician who set me an example as an author, particularly his
"Hand-book and guide to Shetland", and as a predecessor of mine both as a
Shetland Islands Councillor and Chairman of the Leisure and Recreation Committee.

Also Gideon Williamson, a fishermen of Scalloway. In July 1993 Gideon, then aged 83,
completed his walk of the entire Mainland of Shetland by walking Calback Ness.

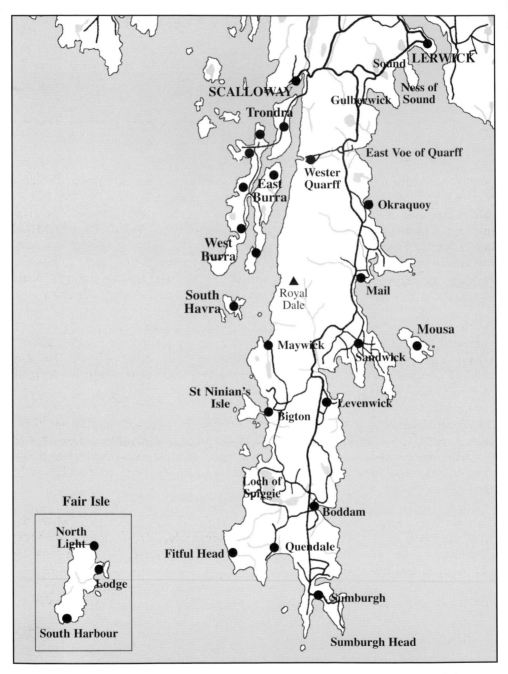

The South Mainland of Shetland showing start and finishing points of the South Mainland way and circular cross-country walks.

Walking the Coastline of Shetland No. 6

SOUTH MAINLAND

78 Miles   (125 Kilometers)

The South Mainland of Shetland has been likened in shape to the blade of a sword. At the pommel on the top of the blade, only a few miles apart, the ancient and modern capitals of Shetland, Scalloway and Lerwick, face the Atlantic and North Sea respectively. It is an area of great contrasts; on the west side the high broodling hills of Clift Sound look down on some of the most fertile land in Shetland. From the rugged splendour of Fitful Head one can survey the sparkling sands in Bay of Quendale. Historic monuments abound with the famous Jarlshof site near Sumburgh now excavated to reveal its secrets. The walker will find many more brochs, iron-age promontory forts and other relics of long ago. There are also many humps, bumps and hollows that may yet reveal finds to rival Jarlshof.

For the moment the walker will have to create in his or her imagination the purpose they once served. The Lochs of Spiggie and Hillwell and the Pool of Virkie are just some of the superb bird watching areas, however, some will find the puffins of Sumburgh Head unbeatable. Inshore sightings of whales and other cetacean have increased considerably off South Mainland in recent years.

The South Mainland way stretches from Scalloway to Lerwick and the first part of the book presents it as a long distance footpath. However, some of the linear walks are well suited to 'there and back' walks and you see the same scenery from a different perspective. If a combination of car and cycle use is utilised, as I do, then the linear walks can be achieved independently of any support.

The second part suggests several loop or circular walks as well as covering walking the coastline of East and West Burra, Trondra, St. Ninian's Isle, Fair Isle, Mousa and South Havra. There will never be a dull moment wherever you decide to tramp in South Mainland and the islands which lie off it.

Good walking!

Peter Guy

WALKING THE COASTLINE OF SHETLAND NO. 6

SOUTH MAINLAND

78 Miles (125 Kilometres)

Section	From	To	Miles	(Kms)	Hrs	Page
1	SCALLOWAY	WESTER QUARFF	3.5	5.5	2	13
2	WESTER QUARFF	MAYWICK	7.5	11.5	4	15
3	MAYWICK	BIGTON	3.5	5.5	2	19
4	BIGTON	QUENDALE	10	16	5	21
5	QUENDALE	SUMBURGH HOTEL	6	9.5	3	25
6	SUMBURGH HOTEL	BODDAM	9	14.5	5	31
7	BODDAM	LEVENWICK	6	9.5	3	35
8	LEVENWICK	SANDWICK	5	8	3	39
9	SANDWICK	MAIL	7	11	4	43
10	MAIL	OKRAQUOY	7	11	4	47
11	OKRAQUOY	EAST VOE OF QUARFF	3	5	2	51
12	EAST VOE OF QUARFF	GULBERWICK	3	5	2	53
13	GULBERWICK	SOUND	3.5	5.5	2	56
14	SOUND	LERWICK MARKET CROSS	4	6.5	2	59
	TOTAL		**78**	**125**	**43**	

CIRCULAR WALKS

Section	From	To	Miles	(Kms)	Hrs	Page
A	ST NINIAN'S ISLE		3.5	5.5	2	61
B	IRELAND	Maywick	5	8	2.5	65
C	MOSQUITO MEMORIAL ROYL DALE		5	8	3	67
D	SOUTH HAVRA ISLAND		2.5	4	2	70
E	LOCH OF SPIGGIE		5	8	2.5	73
F	FITFUL HEAD		6	10	4	75
G	SUMBURGH HEAD		2.5	4	2	78
H	SANDWICK	Noness	6	9.5	3	81
I	MOUSA ISLAND		4	6.5	3	83
J	NESS OF SOUND		3	5	2	85
K	TRONDRA		6.5	11	3	89
L	WEST BURRA	Hamnavoe	3.5	5.5	2	91
M	WEST BURRA	Papil	4	6.5	2	93
N	WEST BURRA	Kettla Ness	5	8	3	97
O	WEST BURRA	Brunna Ness	2	3	1	100
P	EAST BURRA	Wester Heog	3.5	5.5	2	103
Q	EAST BURRA	Houss Ness	5	8	3	105
R	FAIR ISLE LODGE	South Harbour	5	8	3	106
S	FAIR ISLE LODGE	North Light	5	8	3	109

Be Prepared

Have a knowledge of basic First Aid.

Know how to navigate properly using map and compass.

Carry the OS map (maps) appropriate to the walk being undertaken.

Select the right equipment for walking. Carry waterproofs, spare sweater, whistle, food, torch, gloves and balaclava.

Leave word of your planned walk and report your return.

Respect the land

Take care not to drop litter. It is unsightly and can be dangerous to animals.

Remember to use gate or stiles where possible instead of climbing fences and walls.
Park with consideration, remembering that agricultural vehicles may need access near where you leave a car.

Keep dogs under full control. Remember, crofters are entitled to shoot dogs found worrying sheep.

Be weatherwise

Exercise caution in low cloud or mist.

On cliffs windy and misty conditions can create dangerous situations.

Aim to complete a walk in daylight hours.

One hazard, noted by John Reid (1869) can be met in the peat hills where there can be, "dismal trenches filled with stagnant water into which many a luckless traveller has stepped unwittingly", so, both on the banks and in the hills, "Watch your feet!"

MAPS

Ordnance Survey (OS) maps are essential aids to safe walking in South Mainland, as elsewhere. There are two suitable scales of map available:

Landranger series   1:50,000   1¼ in to 1 mile   2cm to 1km

Sheet 4	Shetland	South Mainland (revised September 1998 to February 1999)

For greater detail use **Pathfinder series**   1:25,000

Sheet	HU 44/54	Lerwick
	HU 33/43/53	Scalloway
	HU 32/42	Sandwick (Shetland) and Mousa
	HU 31/41	Sumburgh
	HY 75/85	North Rondaldsay and Fair Isle

A NOTE ON SOME HISTORICAL ACCOUNTS OF THE SOUTH MAINLAND OF SHETLAND

Throughout history many people have made their first landfall in Shetland in the South Mainland, some by sea at Grutness Voe or by air at Sumburgh Airport. First impressions have sometimes been influenced by the elation felt by visitors at surviving the passage north and then finding such a pleasant country awaiting them. Comments therefore tend to be most favourable:

John Brand (1701)
"In this parish (Dunrossness) are several very good Voes or Harbours commodious for ships to ride in. In this there is also much corn-land, the ground bearing the Richest Grain in many places not so Mossy and covered over with Heath, as other parishes are, which makes them to have less fewel, the more corn ...... the land lying so low and sandy in many places is convenient for conies (rabbits) which abound here about the Ness. In this parish there is a great fishing."

George Low (1774)
"To the northward of Fitful Head the country puts on a more beautiful appearance. Fine fields of corn intermixed with meadow and pasture grounds, here and there a loch or other piece of water, all contribute to render this side the most desirable part of Shetland."

Sir Walter Scott (1814) enjoyed himself climbing Fitful Head.
"It would have been a fine situation to compose an ode to the 'Genius of Sumburgh Head' or an 'Elegy upon a Cormorant' but I gave vent to my excited feelings in a more simple way; and sitting gently down on the steep green slope which led to the beach I e'en slid down a few hundred feet and found the exercise quite an adequate vent to my enthusiasm."

Samuel Hibbert (1822) landed at Grutness and thought that, "nothing is indeed wanting but a few trees to complete the picture of fertility". Various writers comment on the liveliness of the men of Cunningsburgh and Hibbert also seems similarly impressed: "Nor is the hardy race of people named Coningsburghers that inhabit this district said to be less wild than the rugged soil from which they derive their support."

Christian Ployen (1840) on his visit to "the farthest north and most inclement point of the empire" enjoyed a great welcome, "Shetlanders are indeed noted for hospitality and attention to strangers and they certainly do deserve this character". He was particularly interested in Burra Isle where he found, "Immense heaps of cured fish lay on the beach and a number of women and old men were busy stacking what was not fully dry, as the sky threatened rain."

John Reid (1869) found the crofts of Dunrossness better cultivated and noted that "in all Dunrossness, an extensive parish, there is not a single house licensed to sell spirituous liquors." Departure was not easy, "After a succession of gales, which detained me two weeks at Sumburgh, waiting a favourable opportunity to make a passage to Fair Isle, succeeded a day of perfect calm." However it was "Three nights after the weather enabled us to make a second start."

John Tudor (1883) enjoyed tramping through Dunrossness, "A very beautiful walk it is too, full of exquisite views, from the largest-sized landscape down to little cabinet gems, that you would keep, if transferred to water-colours, for your own sanctum." How he would have enjoyed the invention of photography! He enjoyed Easter Quarff; "here a valley cuts right through the range of hills that constitute the backbone of this portion of the Mainland. Across this valley boats were once – may still be – drawn from sea to sea." He preferred to walk because the "rate of progression", of the horses he was given, "is about that of the 'Dead March' in 'Saul'".

Dr Mortimer Manson (1932) suggests that, "capital fun can be got clambering out over the half-mile of steep broken rocks at the end of Scatness, from where one can hear and see the 'dinning' and swirl of the Roost." (The Sumburgh Roost is the conflict of two tides from the east and west of Shetland creating a three-mile wide race of broken water. It can have quite an impact on shipping passing through the area.)

Dr Manson points out that Dunrossness is, "The meeting place of antiquity and modernity, for at Sumburgh Airport, which serves the whole of Shetland, aeroplanes take off and alight within a few hundred yards of the now famous Jarlshof excavations."

Walk 1: SCALLOWAY – WESTER QUARF

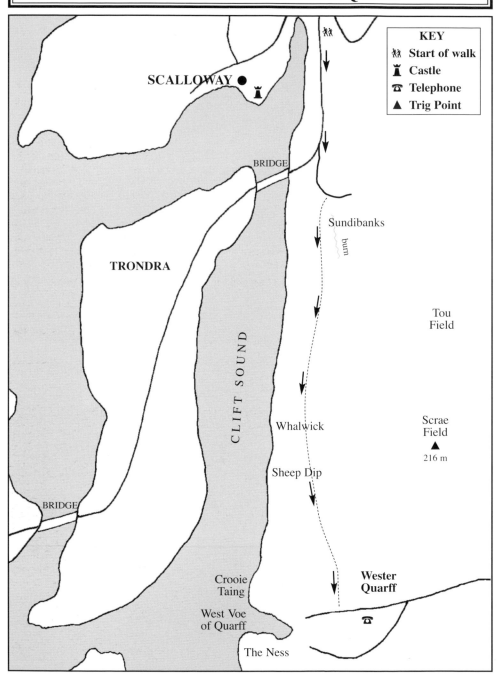

KEY

👫	**Start of walk**
♜	**Castle**
☎	**Telephone**
▲	**Trig Point**

SCALLOWAY ●

BRIDGE

Sundibanks

burn

TRONDRA

Tou Field

C L I F T   S O U N D

Whalwick

Scrae Field
▲
216 m

Sheep Dip

BRIDGE

Crooie Taing

Wester Quarff

☎

West Voe of Quarff

The Ness

WALK 1: SCALLOWAY – WESTER QUARFF ▰▰▰▰

3½ miles (5.6 kms) : 2 hours

OS Maps: **Landranger Sheet 4 Shetland – South Mainland**
Pathfinder Sheet 33/43/53 Scalloway

A magnificent introduction to the South Mainland walk combining views of 'bonny Scalloway' and its busy harbour with those to be enjoyed when high above Clift Sound. Trondra, East and West Burra will be seen in their entirety from the hills as well as much more of Shetland's west coast. This is also an ideal linear walk returning to Scalloway during the course of an afternoon. Avoid a misty day.

Leave Scalloway by walking the paved road which heads south along East Voe of Scalloway to the bridge to Trondra and subsequently West and East Burra. There are good views of the harbour, which is usually busy with the activities of fishing boats and Scalloway Castle on Blacks Ness. At the top of the hill before the main road descends to the Trondra bridge turn left up a road marked Sundibanks. Pass a variety of smart modern houses in contrast to the traditional neat croft, which survives amongst them at Easterhoull. Walk down to the two small crofts at the end of the road and tucked into the folds of the hill noting a track, which snakes up the hill behind them. To get to this track turn right in the turning circle where a sign says 'No vehicles beyond here' and cross a concrete bridge and make for a pebbly beach. The track goes between two grassy knolls to cross the Burn of Sundibanks courtesy of an old trailer. No sign of a water mill (one might expect to find a ruin just upstream) here or further up. This burn flows through a miniature gorge where ferns and heather grow in profusion and boasts a lovely collection of miniature rapids, pools and races. It is easier; however, to walk the hard core cart track up to a field gate where it becomes a grass track and meanders up the hill. Snipe abound.

Sundibanks.

13

Quarff – West Voe ('Purgatory')   J. D. Rattar (circa 1925)

Below us the whole of the island of Trondra is laid out to view. Follow a line of redundant fencing posts to the near the top of this hill from which is a view which includes salmon cages, both square and circular, dotted around in the voes. We are now above Whal Wick and to our east the Trg. Pt. Of Scrae Field 216m stands on the hill. More prominent are the ruins of two buildings, for this hill was once used for communications and was the site of the receiving and transmitting station of the 'beam' radio telephone from Shetland to Scotland in the 1930s.

Two houses on the ness of West Voe of Quarff come into view with a line of boats hauled up below them. Walk up to the tongue of the next hill by crossing a small field gate in a fence and look down, west, on to the last area of reasonably flat pasture land on the sea shore. By looking east we can now see the east coast of Mainland and houses in Easter Quarff are visible. If the weather is at all reasonable it is the view south which is totally captivating as the Clift Hills get even higher and the far horizon is bordered by Fitful Head.

Cross a fence and descend to Wester Quarff where we cross the burn and climb up to the road.

WALK 2: WESTER QUARFF – MAYWICK

7½ miles (11.5 kms) : 4 hours

OS Maps: **Landranger Sheet 4 Shetland – South Mainland**
Pathfinder Sheets 33 Scalloway
                              32 Sandwick

This walk involves hill climbing on rough terrain and includes Royl Field (293m), the highest hill in the South Mainland walk. The main threat is mist, which can appear on the tops without warning and can hang about there for some time. Make sure you carry a compass and keep well to the east of the cliff edges. The walk includes views of South Havra and a memorial to the crew of a RAF Mosquito, which crashed in 1944.

In the delightfully sheltered settlement of Wester Quarff note protected vegetation thrives, wild flowers pack the roadside verges and the delightfully named house Beneath-a-burn nestles at the foot of the Glen of Quarff; the lovely little waterfall and pool nearby is well worth seeking out in the Burn of the Glen of Quarff.

Take the road west to The Ness. The Ness, according to black humour tradition, was once known as 'Purgatory'. In the days when Burra, Quarff and Bressay shared a minister some deceased Bressay people were taken to Papil on Burra for burial. They would be brought to this staging post Ness to await conveyance by boat across Clift Sound! Commence the climb to Muskna Field by walking up the shoulder of the hill behind the house. Below are the remains of Roberts' Crooie and, further on, Spencies' Toon, a cultivated area and dwelling of a man, tradition tells, who drowned his wife in Clift Sound but escaped justice by fleeing the area. The walk now becomes the longest at high level that one can do in Shetland.

The succession of hills give one a series of spectacular views which, with the changes of light, often change dramatically quite often. The highest hill in South Mainland is Royl Field where there is a Trg. Pt. 293m. Below it, west on a shoulder of the cliff on Royl Dale, is the memorial and surviving wreckage of an

Clift Sound and Clift Hills from North House (East Burra).

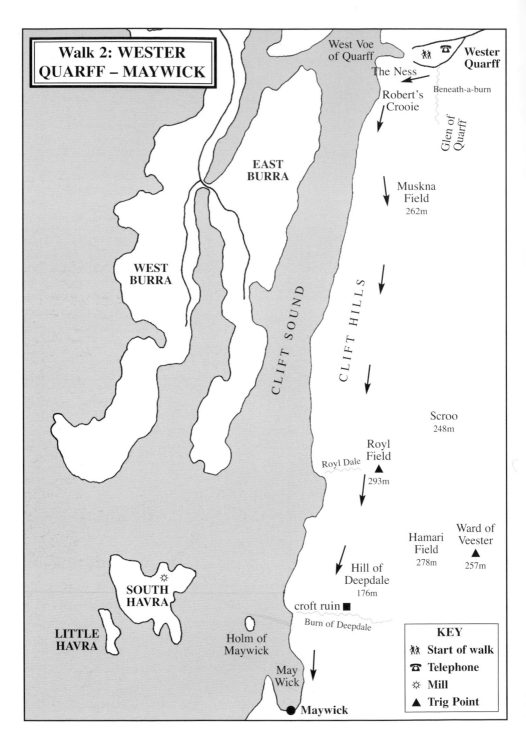

Walk 2: WESTER QUARFF – MAYWICK

West Voe of Quarff

Wester Quarff

The Ness

Beneath-a-burn

Robert's Crooie

Glen of Quarff

EAST BURRA

Muskna Field
262m

WEST BURRA

CLIFT SOUND

CLIFT HILLS

Scroo
248m

Royl Dale

Royl Field
▲
293m

Hamari Field
278m

Ward of Veester
▲
257m

Hill of Deepdale
176m

SOUTH HAVRA

croft ruin ■

Burn of Deepdale

LITTLE HAVRA

Holm of Maywick

May Wick

● Maywick

KEY

乑	**Start of walk**
☎	**Telephone**
☼	**Mill**
▲	**Trig Point**

RAF Mosquito aircraft. Walk down to the memorial; the full story is told in Circular Walk No. C.

Royl Dale was the scene of 'The Battle of the Floss' on 12th August 1771 (floss is the silky fibre obtained from cotton grass and was used, amongst other things, for making ropes). It could be gathered in Royl Dale from dawn on 12th August each year by the folk from Burra and Cunningsburgh. In 1771 the Cunningsburgh folk set off in the middle of the night only to find that when they arrived at dawn the Burra folk had harvested all the floss during the night and were about to leave. There was subsequently quite a scuffle!

From the Mosquito return up the slopes and walk south to Bonxa Hill – a reminder of how popular the Cliff Hills are with the great skuas, or bonxies – after which the slopes of the hills become a little less steep. All of the islands of South Havra, with its ruined windmill prominent, and Little Havra are in view. Descend the slopes of Hill of Deepdale above the Holm of Maywick and reach the Burn of Deepdale. Here will be found on the burn's northern slope a small ruined stone building with a stone wall 50ft in length adjacent to it (a sheep shelter?). Tradition tells of a lock-up being established in Deepdale where miscreants from Sandwick could be put to reflect on their crimes. It is possible that so called 'leper houses' also stood in this dale. Depressions in the ground indicate that there have been other buildings but there are no traces of them now. Visible from this building up the green valley, where the burn is often choked with a profusion of lilies, the ruins of Deepdale croft are visible on the skyline.

From Deepdale climb up SW to a new wire fence erected on the cliff edge. The beach of Maywick is now visible and if the tide is out so is the sandy beach on the Taing. Continue along the wire fence admiring the dramatic cliff scenery complete with caves. A challenging deep gorge now has to be crossed. The fence makes it, so must we though you might find it easier to go inland and cross by an old fence. Once over the burn go through a metal gate and walk down to an old car track. This passes a small skeo once used for drying fish as "it's the windiest part of the Maywick", explained Jennifer Sutherland who was restoring it as a shelter the day I walked by.

Walk into the small sheltered community of Maywick where helpful signs guide one to the beach.

Maywick.

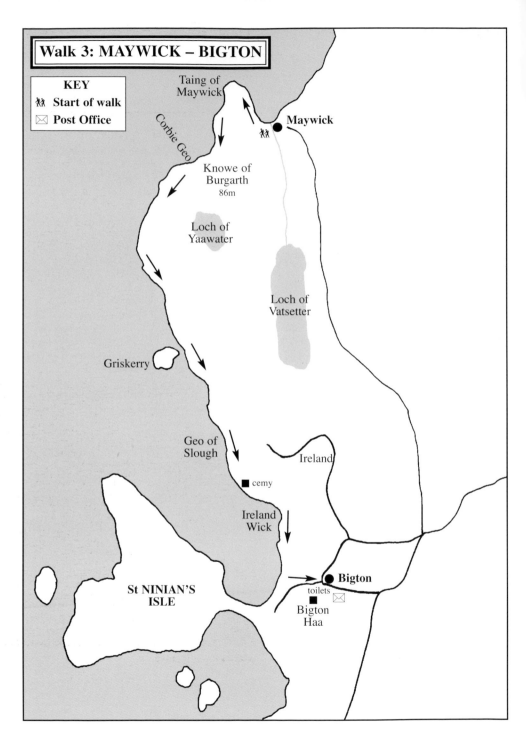

Walk 3: MAYWICK – BIGTON

KEY
Start of walk
Post Office

Taing of
Maywick

Maywick

Corbie Geo

Knowe of
Burgarth
86m

Loch of
Yaawater

Loch of
Vatsetter

Griskerry

Geo of
Slough

Ireland

cemy

Ireland
Wick

Bigton

toilets

Bigton
Haa

St NINIAN'S
ISLE

WALK 3: MAYWICK – BIGTON

3½ miles (5 kms) : 2 hours

OS Maps: **Landranger Sheet 4 Shetland – South Mainland**
                Pathfinder Sheet 32 Sandwick

Maywick is a lovely haven to reach after tramping the wilds of the Clift Hills. The road runs south from the bay to the Bigton road past Loch of Vatsetter. The coastal route takes in some impressive scenery and then the cultivated areas round Ireland and Bigton.

The small Maywick community enjoys a sheltered sand and shingle beach surrounded by quartz veined cliffs. There is a privacy about this hidden spot and it can all look serenely beautiful. However , a reminder of the cruelty of the sea can be seen in the shape of a headstone on the cliff edge above the west end of the beach. It reads, 'In memory of Laurence Smith the beloved husband of Andrena Yonson. He was drowned at the ling fishing 27 Jan, 1857, Aged 44 years. Erected by his sons.' Continue up the cliffs to a high spot on the Knowe of Burgarth (86m) where impressive cliff scenery begins again at Corbie Geo and continues round to Burgi Stacks. There is a striking stack at Griskerry from which walk down and round attractive Geo of Slough. A gradual descent brings us down to the cemetery below the emerald green of Ireland.

Here are magnificent views of Bigton Wick, the sandy tombola between Bigton and St. Ninian's Isle and the coastline beyond. A gated track brings one to the road end in Ireland from which we cross Ireland Wick, cross some fields on the edge of the banks and reach Bigton on an access road to some farm buildings. Alternatively take the road which links the car park for St. Ninian's Isle with the village. Bigton is a very pleasant spot with a Post Office/Shop, St. Ninian's Church (1905) and Community Hall, all enjoying some protection from the elements given by the Ward of Scousburgh, on top of

which is a Trg. Pt. 263m, a cairn and a variety of masts which can be seen on the skyline. Bigton Haa and its associated buildings stand out to the south. The Haa was built in 1788 by John Bruce-Stewart whose initials and date are inscribed on the moulded architrave to the blocked up former entrance.

Maywick – cliff grave.

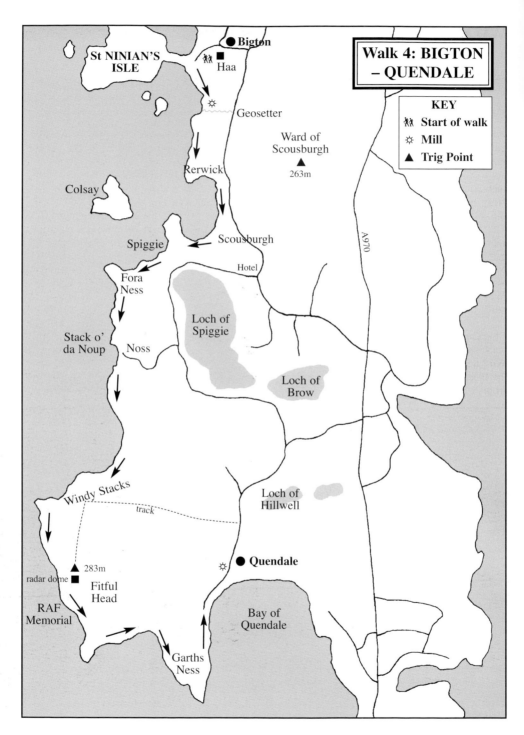

● Bigton
Haa
St NINIAN'S ISLE
Geosetter
Ward of Scousburgh
▲ 263m
Rerwick
Colsay
Spiggie
Scousburgh
Hotel
Fora Ness
Loch of Spiggie
Stack o' da Noup
Noss
Loch of Brow
Windy Stacks
track
Loch of Hillwell
radar dome ■
▲ 283m
Fitful Head
Quendale
RAF Memorial
Bay of Quendale
Garths Ness

Walk 4: BIGTON – QUENDALE

KEY

👫 **Start of walk**
☼ **Mill**
▲ **Trig Point**

WALK 4: BIGTON – QUENDALE

10 miles (16 kms) : 5 hours

| OS Maps: | Landranger Sheet 4 Shetland – South Mainland |
| | Pathfinder Sheet 31 Sumburgh |

Another long stretch of coastline with no large communities after Scousburgh until Quendale is reached. Many walkers will want to spend time at Loch of Spiggie but few will want to miss the increasingly dramatic cliff scenery from Fora Ness and up Fitful Head. Avoid walking on misty days.

Leave Bigton by taking the track down to the car park and interpretive display board for St. Ninian's Isle. The walk to this island, linked to the mainland by the spectacular tombola, and round it takes about two hours and a full description will be found in Circular Walk A.

Climb up the sandy cliff from the beach and walk south where the fields in summer have Wild Seabriors growing in profusion. One of the most delightful spots on this walk will be from where the Burn of Geosetter, having

passed the most attractive green roofed white painted walled croft bearing its name, tumbles vigorously down into the geo. Nature in profusion provides a backdrop for the burn as it passes under a footbridge made of an old quern and a ruined water mill. Entrance to this scene is through a ruined gateway which, with its dressed stone gate hinges, harks back to a period of some splendour.

Just beyond here is where the photograph of the derelict tractor was taken. The houses clustered round Rerwick come into view. We round the Ness of Rerwick into the Bay of Scousburgh where the sandy beach provides a haven for boats, sea birds and seals. Climb up from the beach and onto the road. Admire the clearness of the water and hopefully the antics of the seals who frequent this delightful little bay. Here I once was captivated by the sight of a young seal

Tombola at St. Ninian's Isle.

"It's work done" old tractor, Ness of Rerwick.

leaping like a dolphin out of the water as it crossed the bay, played with a lobster creel float and then hauled itself up on to the beach to recover from its exertions!

Walk the road until you have passed a concrete wartime sentry post cut into the side of the hill opposite a deep geo. Go through a gate and descend across the fields towards the large beach passing a stone windbreak. Caravans cluster in the dunes behind the beach and from there it is worth a diversion south to the road and RSPB Interpretive Display Board on the north shore of the Loch of Spiggie.

The village of Scousburgh which lies above the loch has accommodation and fine views of the surrounding countryside and coast. No remains are now visible of the broch from which it takes its name (thought to have been on a high conical knoll in the middle of the village). What can be seen, just, are the scant remains of a broch on the small island in the Loch of Brow. At Lunabister is the site of another broch which, when it was dug into, revealed a number of relics including a trough-quern. These broch sites are the first we have found since leaving Scalloway.

The Loch of Spiggie is renowned for good trout fishing and with the Loch of Brow is an important Nature Reserve. In summer the lochs host only a few wading birds and provide a bathing facility for arctic terns and skuas. In winter, however, they have attracted up to 400 whooper swans, grey lag geese, golden eye, wigeon, teals, large flocks of pochard and in spring up to 50 long tailed ducks gather to roost.

Return to the popular Scousburgh sands beach and go round Northern Ness, from which are excellent views of the island of Colsay with its prehistoric cairn. Follow the cliffs down to Spiggie Bay – one of the most scenic and photogenic in Shetland. There is a tarred roof

Seals on beach, Rerwick.

Spiggie beach.

boathouse by some ancient noosts and a slipway to help boat access to the beach. The red cliffs rise each side of the beach from the middle of which is an excellent view up Muckle Sound of Foula on the far horizon. A most romantic spot.

From the beach at Spiggie cross the road bridge and head up the cliffs to the right of the house. Where a stone wall joins an earth embankment note a small standing stone, about 3ft high which in certain conditions one can imagine carvings on it. It is comfortable walking with no fences across the grazing area on Fora Ness but take care round Longi Geo. Here are more excellent views of the loch and sheepfold on the island of Colsay. Mammals and birds are remembered in the naming of Whale Geo and Corbie Geo. The busy croft of Noss nestles below a plateau from which one climbs the Noup of Noss and the dramatic Stack o' da Noup, joined to the Noup by a striking cliff ridge. The stacks running out to form Landvillas and Swarta Skerry boast a natural arch. As one climbs round Wick of Shunni we pass some hardstanding and other ruins of World War II army buildings. Many more can be seen across Noss Hill and Scalla Field. Climb up above The Windy Stacks, which often

live up to their name, and one may be tempted to take the road up to the radar dome. Otherwise continue round The Nev which is renowned for its caves, particularly one named Thief's House. The final ascent to the top is quite demanding but one can pause to view a very ruined croft building and the cliffs, particularly red where there has been substantial topsoil erosion. There is an incredible vista, which includes all the way up the west coast of Mainland Shetland. The going is made tougher by having to surmount the many remains of earth embankments (fealie dykes) on the slopes of the hill.

The dome at the top houses a radar, which has a radius of 200 miles, and with adjacent radio station are part of Sumburgh Airport installations.

The cliff scenery round majestic Fitful Head is most dramatic and from the top of the cliff you will hopefully enjoy a view of both Foula and Fair Isle.

Pass the Trig. Pt. (283m) and continue along the cliff top where on reaching a metal strainer drop down onto a small plateau. Here stands a stone memorial, erected by the community council, which replaced an earlier wooden cross, inscribed:

To the seven crew of RAF Halifax bomber R9438(H) of 35 Squadron RAF who crashed into the cliffs here on returning from an air raid on the German pocket battleship 'Tirpitz' 30/31st March 1942.

Walk further along the top of the Head to overlook Whales Wick and a cluster of stacks including Ripack. Descend the slopes to Garths Ness where in the geo below the tanker 'Braer' was grounded in 1993. Today no sign of the tanker is visible.

The island of Noss is visible from the top of this Ness and you can choose either to cut across past the extensive croft ruins of Garthbanks to the Bay of Quendale or aim for the square building at the bottom of the SE slope of the Ness. The building was built for a Ministry of Defense installation and a MoD road connects it to Quendale.

The sandy beach of Quendale is very popular in summer and just beyond the beach and a derelict Haa is the large 19th century Quendale Mill. This is a beautifully restored example of an old water mill with a vertical wheel. It is well worth a visit as the history of the mill is graphically illustrated and you can see the original working mechanism. To the north of Bay of Quendale is Loch of Hillwell, another important bird watching loch. At Breck of Quendale a Pictish symbol stone was found, now in the Shetland Museum, Lerwick.

There has been a great deal of speculation about what may lie under the sandy links of Quendale for this was once good arable land. Many prehistoric relics have been found and near Garthbanks in 1830, a hoard of silver armlets and Anglo-Saxon coins of Ethelred, Athelstan, Edwy and Eadgar was unearthed – so keep your eyes open! Today you are more likely to see a replica of the Quendale Beast. This was a representation of a winged animal (without head or foreleg) found in 1931 east of Quendale chapel site. Only half of the bronze open work was found (and since lost), thought to be a

The Quendale Beast.   **Jack Rae**

harness ornament. Jack Rae of Shetland Jewellery, designed a piece of jewellery which aims to match the original. There is one burnt mound site on the Links of Quendale. It is oval 18m x 11m x 2m.

Above the beach only a mound now marks the site of the Cross kirk and burial ground as the shifting sands made upkeep difficult and it was abandoned in 1790. Three 17th century inscribed tombstones were moved to the museum at Jarlshof. The latin inscription on one of them is elegiac and reads beautifully:

"Here in the hope of blessed resurrection rest in peace the bones and ashes of one of the best of women, Mistress Barbara Sinclair, sprung from famous stock, as being the eldest daughter of Master John Sinclair of Quendale; graced with exemplary virtue; also the most devoted wife of the Worthy Master Hector Bruce of Muness and thrice-happy mother of a family of richest promise, who died amid grief profound and universal on the 22nd of the month of May in the year 1675, the 38th of year age."

The wording on the stone reflects on a strata of society in Shetland in the 1600s. Note the use of Latin; the epitaph is thought to have been composed by William Neven of Windhouse, Yell. The style of the design evidently suggests that the stone may have been carved in the Low Countries.

WALK 5: QUENDALE – SUMBURGH HOTEL ███████

6 miles (9.5 kms) : 3 hours

OS Maps: **Landranger Sheet 4 Shetland – South Mainland**
Pathfinder Sheet 31 Sumburgh

A walk dominated by Scat Ness, with its Iron Age forts and activity at Sumburgh Airport. Easy walking and excellent sea bird watching in West Voe of Sumburgh.

Leave the beach at Quendale and follow the low-level banks below Ward Hill, Erne's Ward and Toab to reach the main road heading for Sumburgh. On a flat shoulder WSW of the highest point of Ward Hill are two concentric circles of unhewn stones set close together. One academic described them as; 'a most interesting example of an Astronomical Temple erected for the worship of the Sun-god'. The Inventory disputes this! Leave the road once past the runway approach and follow the coast opposite Little Holm and Lady's Holm. Both holms attract bird life and one can wonder if one of the holms is where, tradition tells, there was once a circular fence of stones. In the enclosed space ordeal by single combat took place in Viking times. The large Loch of Gards is surrounded by planti-crubs, the first we have seen for some time. Walk along the top of a large bank of stones behind, which are walls and enclosures, including a stone boat noost. After the embankment stone wall ramparts stretch to the Hog of Breigeo. Here are two circular stone enclosures, one with a depression in the middle of it. It was here at Fraga that a Bronze Age burial chamber was discovered. A cist containing a complete human skeleton was discovered during the demolition of a cairn. The burial belonged to the Bronze Age; no relics of metal were found but fragments of a beaker-urn were recovered from the cist. Descend from a rocky outcrop to the boulder-strewn geo and beach noting the large slanting stacks like the slope of a stage. Climb up to a well-constructed stone cairn. Access to the fort at Ness of Burgi is made easier by the provision of a chain railing across a rocky ridge. This is the first, and natural, defence of the fort. Near the fort is an information board giving some information on the well preserved Iron Age promontory fort and adjacent large rectangular cairn of stones, once part of the fort and removed during excavation.

The second line of defense was a rampart of earth and stones bordered by a ditch on both sides pierced by a boulder-flanked passage. The fort was constructed as a rectangular masonry blockhouse and contains three cells pierced by a passage, which is still covered by three of its original massive lintels. The fort was excavated in the 1930s and the blockhouse restored in 1971; behind it no deposits survived and it is bare rock today.

Cairn, Scatness.

Walk 5: QUENDALE – SUMBURGH HOTEL

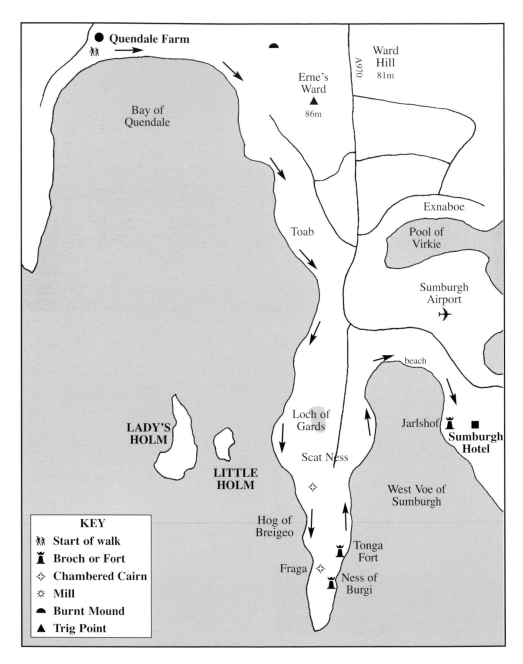

● **Quendale Farm**

Bay of
Quendale

Erne's
Ward
▲
86m

Ward
Hill
81m

A970

Exnaboe

Pool of
Virkie

Toab

Sumburgh
Airport
✈

beach

**LADY'S
HOLM**

Loch of
Gards

Jarlshof ♜ ■ **Sumburgh
Hotel**

**LITTLE
HOLM**

Scat Ness

West Voe of
Sumburgh

KEY
🕴 **Start of walk**
♜ **Broch or Fort**
✧ **Chambered Cairn**
☼ **Mill**
⌒ **Burnt Mound**
▲ **Trig Point**

Hog of
Breigeo

Tonga
Fort ♜

Fraga ✧

Ness of
Burgi ♜

Scatness fort and Fitful Head.

Sea pinks grow on Scat Ness in profusion adding considerable colour, in season, to the site. Walk further west to round the ness to view distant Horse Island and return past a rough stone cairn. At Tonga is a profusion of mounds and ditches with remains of a stone building and on the promontory a row of rough stones. Here protected by a rampart are the remains of another Iron Age promontory fort, a rectangular masonry blockhouse with a single oval cell surviving. Beyond them stands a World War II building and a small loch popular with redshanks and other small waders, a sheep wash and six rough stone boat noosts.

A well-built stone wall runs E-W within, which is an interesting enclosure made up of large stone slabs. Return to the main road either by the shore or by the track, on the right of which near Gards is a stone/concrete slab on which is discernible:

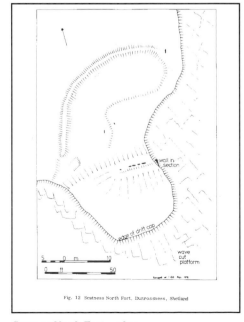

Fig. 12 Scatness North Fort, Dunrossness, Shetland

Scatness North Fort – plan.

Above: Ness of Burgi, access route with guard rail. Below: Ness of Burgi – plan.

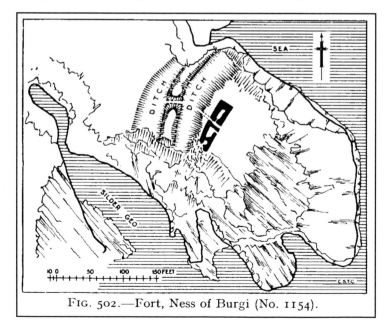

FIG. 502.—Fort, Ness of Burgi (No. 1154).

1945
Erected by Italian PoW for kindness
shown to them by the people of Scat Ness
while serving with the RAF Coastal Command
Cpl Carruthers WR

Walk across the lovely beach of West Voe. Toilets will be found at the east end. Follow the track to the main road and almost immediately turn right up the drive of the Sumburgh Hotel. The hotel offers accommodation (the Fair Isle room is particularly magnificent) and meals. It was once a Bruce mansion and was built in 1867.

Access to the Jarlshof settlement and visitor centre is from the hotel car park. Jarlshof is an internationally famous archaeological site spanning 3000 years of settlement from Neolithic times to the remains of a medieval farmhouse. Sir Walter Scott named the farmhouse Jarlshof in his novel "The Pirate"

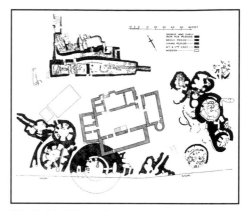

The Jarlshof site – plan.

and the name is now used for the whole site. A visit to this site is not to be missed; there is an interpretive centre (Historic Scotland) and an excellent guidebook is available.

Jarlshof.

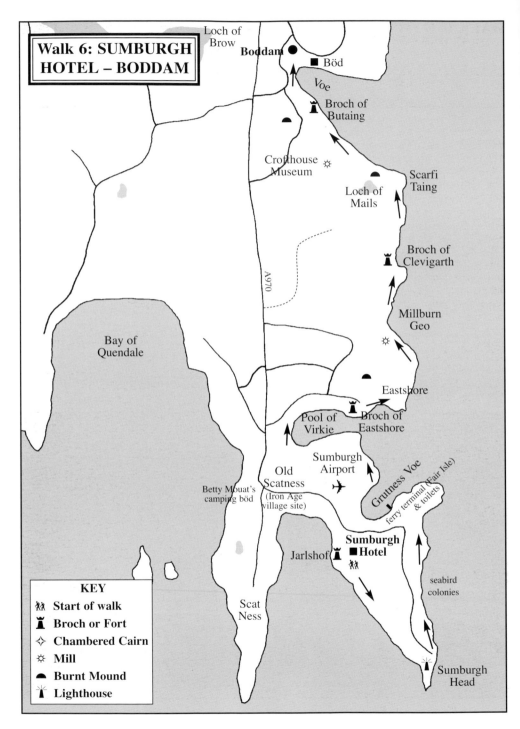

Walk 6: SUMBURGH HOTEL – BODDAM

Loch of Brow
Boddam ●
■ Böd
Voe
Broch of Butaing
Crofthouse Museum ☼
Loch of Mails
Scarfi Taing
Broch of Clevigarth
Millburn Geo
☼
A970
Bay of Quendale
Eastshore
Pool of Virkie
Broch of Eastshore
Betty Mouat's camping böd
Old Scatness (Iron Age village site)
Sumburgh Airport
Grutness Voe
ferry terminal (Fair Isle) & toilets
Jarlshof 🚶 ■ Sumburgh Hotel
seabird colonies
Scat Ness
Sumburgh Head

KEY
🚶 Start of walk
♜ Broch or Fort
◇ Chambered Cairn
☼ Mill
⌒ Burnt Mound
🗼 Lighthouse

WALK 6: SUMBURGH HOTEL – BODDAM

9 miles (14.5 kms) : 5 hours

OS Maps: **Landranger Sheet 4 Shetland – South Mainland**
               Pathfinder Sheet 31 Sumburgh

A walk offering a tremendous variety of attractions. If necessary allow all day. Bird watching on Sumburgh Head and Pool of Virkie, three broch sites and the opportunity to visit the thatched Croft House Museum and restored water mill near Boddam.

On leaving the Sumburgh Hotel first visit the restored wall garden popular with migrating birds and from there cross the fields back to the low banks on the coast. Two tall stone cairns guide one on to a wall, which can be rounded on the cliff edge. Pass another small cairn and a stone wall which incorporates an enclosure at the seaward end of it. On the approach to the next wall head up the hill and cross open grazing ground to join the road which goes to Sumburgh Head lighthouse. Climb up the hill along the sea wall and in the lighthouse compound make for the farthest corner, beyond the horn and view Sumburgh Head. The lighthouse was built in 1821 by Thomas Stevenson, father of Robert Louis Stevenson. The scenic cliffs of the Head have large sea bird colonies, which can be seen by standing on convenient ledges along the wall. The RSPB display board tells of the puffins (2000 pairs in the Sumburgh colony), guillemots, fulmars, shags, kittiwakes and razorbills, that can be viewed from here during the breeding season.

Sumburgh Head is also and excellent place to look out for whales and down the hill at the main car park is an information board and part of the huge skull of a sperm whale on display.

Now leave the road and climb up to the radar station near Compass Head. Keep well away from the cliff edge and make for a stone wall. Between this wall and the next the cliff has walled ramparts but it is the majestic cliff which really catches the eye. Go round the radome

Broch, Eastshore, and croft ruin.

and descend the slope past a war time shelter to reach a cairn on the pebbly beach at Grutness. A telephone box and toilets will be found at the jetty at Grutness Voe, which is the ferry terminal for Fair Isle.

Join the road at the junction of lighthouse and Grutness roads, pausing to admire a lovely garden and note a lighthouse related building, which proudly proclaims on a gatepost:

'To Lighthouse
1 mile
and 1033 yards'

To the NE, on the shore, the area between Grutness and Laward is strewn with massive lumps of rock thrown up in the great gale of 1900. It is now a case of following the main road past the Sumburgh Hotel (do not take the road to the Airport passenger terminal) and walking round the airport perimeter. Before reaching the wig-wag lights look out for a sign on the right hand side of the road showing the access track to the Camping Bod in Betty Mouat's cottage and adjacent Iron Age village site at Old Scatness.

The Shetland Amenity Trust, under the banner of "See the Iron Age come alive", open old Scatness Broch to visitors during part of the summer. The full story of Betty Mouat's epic, single handed, involuntary sail to Norway in 1886 will be found in Dr Mortimer Manson's book "Drifting Alone to Norway".

Leave the main road to turn east to Eastshore, which lies beside the Pool of Virkie, an inter-tidal sand and mudflat. It is one of the most important feeding sites for resident, migrating and vagrant waders. One of the most vagrant was a solitary flamingo which visited the Pool in 1988.

Somewhere between the Pool and Grutness Voe tradition tells that on the Links of Sumburgh a long running feud between Shetland men and the men of Lewis ended in a final battle. The Lewis men are supposed to have been annihilated and there were no more summer raiding parties from the Outer Hebrides.

At Eastshore the harbour and marina of the Ness Boating Club will be found. This was the venue for a lunch I was privileged to arrange for

Croft House Museum, Boddam.

the Shetland Islands Council when the Duke of Edinburgh and the Prince of Wales came to visit Shetland following the grounding of the 'Braer'. The Prince, besieged by reporters more interested in his domestic life, gratefully made the sanctuary of this splendid club. Over lunch he looked at the Viking longship on my Sullom Voe tie and said, "at least that hasn't sunk'.

Above the club stand two small ruined croft houses – fine examples with walls, fire places and window lintels all made up of large rough stones still complete. The Eastshore settlement includes the broch, which has part of its stonework still visible. It is much damaged but close to the beach a chamber can be seen. From the broch a pebbly slipway leads down to the sea where two small creeks would have provided harbour facilities. Make for the Point of Tangpool across gently sloping grazing land noting a Homestead site above. Cross over a wall where the stone cliffs slope to the sea, a popular place for shags. There are planticrubs in profusion in this area, the first large collection we have seen for some time. On top of the next slope is a large stone enclosure with a rectangular cairn in its centre. As we climb to the Taing a long coastal view north emerges but what will probably catch the eye is a natural arch in the ridge cliff before Millburn Geo. The Mill Burn flows down from a marshy area where birds bathe and through the ruins of three watermills, one still in a reasonable state of preservation.

The nameplate of a fishing boat, the 'Pre-Eminence' is embedded into the turf. Just before the next wall are large vertical stones of a Homestead site, which leads one to a boulder strewn area before the wall below the broch. The ridge cliff of shelving rocks, which make up Blo-geo, has a good natural arch. Climb up to the large, well preserved broch of Clevigarth where the outer and inner faces of the wall can still be followed and two cells remain visible. There is a solitary croft ruin above the bay at Broken Brough. The name 'Broken Brough' was given to this mass of rock, which projects from the cliff, because it is not unlike a castle toppling forward into the sea. The high cliffs boast caves and arches but from there descend

Broch, Clevigarth.

to gentler sloping stone cliffs. Near Scarfi Taing is a burnt mound and two stone walls meet. One wall has an opening in it for water to run through after it had driven two water mills. Cross a fence and take the slope with embankments down to the shoreline. The Croft House Museum, with its thatched buildings is now in view and a visit to it is part of this walk.

Aim for an old concrete sheep wash and cross a fence to reach a thatched, restored water mill, the key to which is held in the museum but note how water once fed two mills once working here. Take the well-defined walkway up to a museum, which is well worth a visit. Toilet facilities available here.

To the east of the museum, not far from the edge of the cliffs at Bu Taing near Southvoe are the grass-covered remains of a broch. Three lintel stones remain in position as well as two upright stones. Note that in front of the broch a long high ridge of rock runs parallel to the shore, leaving a narrow lane of water useful for boats. If you prefer to take the road round Northvoe you will pass, unusually, a set of railway signals at 'Columbine' (B&B)! Boddam also has Dunrossness Primary School below which you will pass as you head round the head of the voe. Here the beach is very popular with wading birds when the tide is out. Boddam had a fish curing station and a derelict fishing booth with two floors still stands at Out Voe.

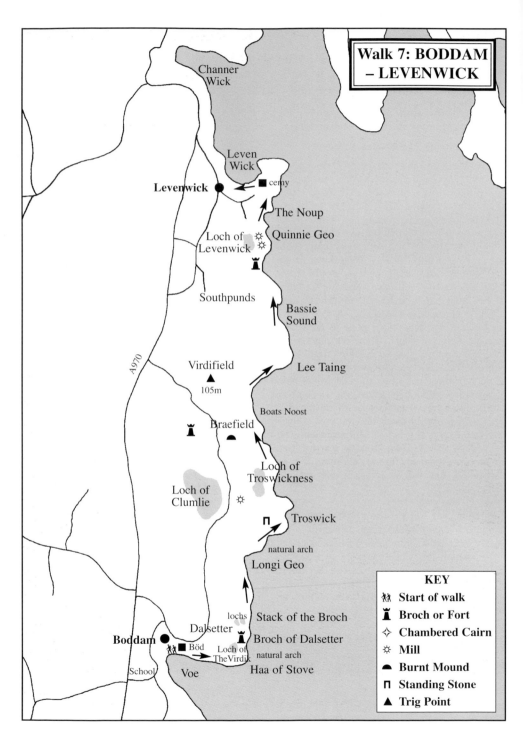

Walk 7: BODDAM – LEVENWICK

Channer Wick

Leven Wick

Levenwick

The Noup

Loch of Levenwick

Quinnie Geo

■ cemy

Southpunds

Bassie Sound

Virdifield

▲ 105m

Lee Taing

Boats Noost

Braefield

Loch of Troswickness

Loch of Clumlie

Troswick

Π

natural arch

Longi Geo

lochs

Stack of the Broch

Dalsetter

Broch of Dalsetter

Boddam ●

Böd

Loch of The Virdik

natural arch

School

Voe

Haa of Stove

A970

KEY

🏃	**Start of walk**
🏰	**Broch or Fort**
✧	**Chambered Cairn**
✿	**Mill**
⬛	**Burnt Mound**
Π	**Standing Stone**
▲	**Trig Point**

WALK 7: BODDAM – LEVENWICK

9 miles (9.5 kms) : 3 hours

OS Maps: Landranger Sheet 4 Shetland – South Mainland
Pathfinder Sheets 31 Sumburgh
32 Sandwick

A fertile stretch of coastline receiving some protection from the elements by the Ward of Scousburgh. Between the sheltered Voe near Boddam to the beautiful sandy bay of Levenwick stand three brochs and impressive standing stone.

We leave Boddam, admiring a well-built dry stone wall and noting a semi-derelict booth with the first objective being the broch of Dalsetter. This can be reached either by following the road up to the housing estate at Dalsetter Wynde, which has a superb prehistoric settlement site on its northern boundary, or via the coast. The coast route starts by going over the second metal gate on the right hand side of the road after the 'Road Narrows' sign. At the point of Haa of Stova is

a 7ft high cairn made up of flat stones. Beyond is a natural arch from which climb up to the magnificent remains of the broch standing in front of some ruined croft buildings. Directly opposite there rises from the sea an isolated mass of rock named Stack of the Brough.

A short length of the outer face of the wall is still recognisable but many out buildings remains are a mystery. Note the two concentric rings of rampart and evidence of there having been two wells just outside the broch. There is no easy access to the sea nearby.

Leave the broch and head past two small lochs to view probably the best example of a natural arch on this stretch of walk at Longi Geo. From here drop down the slopes to the

Broch of Dalsetter and lochs of Longi Geo.

Cairn, Haa of Stova, Boddam.

back to a shipwreck in 1817 but one, of Archibald Smith, who drowned in 1864 salvaging a piece of timber, dates back to 1864. Further along from this tranquil and well tended spot are boat noosts carved into turf banks.

Several ruined water mills lie on the burn as it enters Troswick from the Loch of Clumlie – a loch that boasts a broch ruin in a group of old croft buildings. Only the lower levels of the structure remain. A large embankment of boulders protects Troswick from further incursions by the sea. Behind the embankment the land is very marshy so be prepared for some 'boulder bashing'. Leave the beach through a small gateway to follow the slope up the hill. The flat rocks are a favourite place for seals to bask.

Gorsna Geo with its attendant wedge-shaped stack is our next objective and by a derelict stone windbreak Sandwick comes into view north. Note a 3'x2' stone right on the cliff edge near the loch of Troswick Ness. If the last loch

Troswick – grain dryer.

settlement of Troswick where a small group of houses, one with a grain kiln, nestle above a pebbly beach. The grain mill, where the grain is dried prior to grinding, has been restored by Ian Smith so that he is able to manage corn production from sowing the seed to making flour. The standing stone is prominently placed by a wall before the beach is reached and may have served, amongst other things, as a boundary mark. The irregular block tapes to a point 8ft above the ground. It varies greatly in thickness.

Between the standing stone and the beach where the wall ends stands the solid ruin of a böd, to the north of which are small shards of stone embedded into the slope of the ground facing east. These are gravestones, most dating

Troswick – standing stone with crofts and Scousburgh in background.

(at Broken Brough) looked like a pair of spectacles this next one resembles ping-nez. It is popular with small ducks. Hopefully you are not drooping as you pass the point of this name but fit to descend past Geo of Uin to a Boats Noost. This is an area of flat sloping rocks below Braefield croft and some derelict stone enclosures. The burnt mound also lies on the slope. Some of the large rocks appear to be assembled like cairns. Braefield is an extremely interesting settlement. There is a grain kiln built at the end of a barn and a fine walled garden at the back of the croft house. Braefield has been built on the site of a prehistoric tool factory and examples are still turning up when the earth is ploughed. There is a burnt mound site on Burn of the Rait and further inland, north of Loch of Clumlie, the low levels of a broch survive. When it was excavated in 1887 a clay – sealed cist was discovered within the chamber. The broch ruin is incorporated in the derelict croft buildings but well worth exploring.

Cross a wall to reach rough grazing just the

other side of which is a long cairn made up of flat stones. Lee Taing offers a verdant plateau from which we walk down to ruined buildings by a small loch popular with wading birds. It is

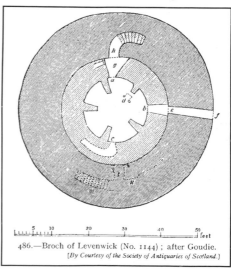

486.—Broch of Levenwick (No. 1144) ; after Goudie.
[By Courtesy of the Society of Antiquaries of Scotland.]

Broch of Levenwick – plan.

very rocky area and there are many stone enclosures. Cross a marshy area to reach the next impressive broch ruin.

The broch of Levenwick stands on a rocky cliff, which descends at a fairly steep angle to the sea. The general outline of the main structure is still clearly visible. When it was first excavated two staircases and a gallery still remained. The great gale of February 1900 did most of the damage. However there are so many ruined stone enclosures it is amazing that any of the broch stones remain. The loch beyond the broch was being visited by a flock of grey lag geese when I passed. Pass the geo Quinnie Geo and where the burn runs through the water lilies the ruins of two water mills will be found. The burn tumbles from these mills into the geo.

A climb brings us onto the Noup topped by a cairn-like knoll below which are some fine stacks and caves. One final climb will take one round Levenwick Ness and down past an old jetty, today used by a flock of eiders, shore windbreak and onto the lovely beach of Levenwick. The cemetery is unusual being situated in a sandy mound. The memorials are mainly Victorian and some, such as the impressive Great War memorial testify to those who gave their lives at sea. The medieval church here was dedicated to St. Leven.

Near the beach at the road end, is a conveniently sited picnic table.

I was once 'caught' picking mushrooms near Levenwick. "You've no right to do so", I was told. Somewhat chastened I replied in mitigation that I came from Yell where anybody could pick mushrooms, anywhere. My interlocutrix was unimpressed, "I have never been to Yell, nor do I ever intend to. So your argument is utter rubbish", she said. Defeated by this logic and speechless I slunk off, but I got to keep the mushrooms.

Broch, Levenwick.

WALK 8: LEVENWICK – SANDWICK

5 miles (8 kms) : 3 hours

OS Maps: **Landranger Sheet 4 Shetland – South Mainland**
Pathfinder Sheet 32 Sandwick

The coastline round the gentle cliffs of Channer Wick, Hos Wick and Sand Wick dominate this walk. Beware fast traffic on the A970 and The Kirn on Cumlewick.

From Levenwick walk up the road to join the A970, leaving it where the crash barrier starts. Walk down the slope of the hill above Moull and onto the footbridge which crosses the Burn of Claver. When this bridge was built in the 1940s sheaves of newspapers were laid across the drying cement. The paper has since petrified leaving text outlined on the stone. At the north end of the beach of Channerwick is a small, roofless, interdenominational chapel which was used until 1953. However, the pews were never removed so the place has rather an eerie feel about it. Amidst lush vegetation another footbridge will be found to take one over the Burn of Channerwick. Head east up the slopes below the croft of Rompa and walk the rugged cliffs to Stemi Geo and round the Ness of Hoswick and its attendant stack, The Berg. Walk below a line of crofts on the way into the well-sheltered Bay of Hos Wick. From the sandy beach a path leads up to Hoswick village where Lawrence J Smith knitting company is established. Opposite this

Sandwick looking towards Hoswick: local peddlar James Petrie.   **James Manson 1906**

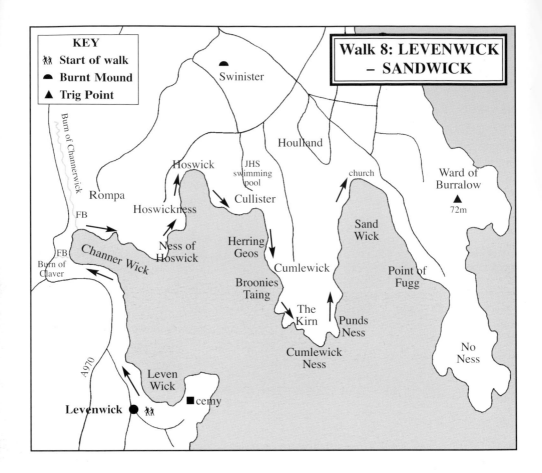

KEY

  Start of walk

  Burnt Mound

  Trig Point

Swinister

Burn of Channerwick

Houlland

Hoswick

JHS swimming pool

church

Ward of Burralow

72m

Rompa

Hoswickness

Cullister

FB

Ness of Hoswick

Herring Geos

Sand Wick

FB

Channer Wick

Burn of Claver

Cumlewick

Point of Fugg

Broonies Taing

The Kirn

Punds Ness

No Ness

A970

Cumlewick Ness

Leven Wick

cemy

Levenwick

is Da Warp and Weft Visitor Centre and Tearoom. Further up the hill stands the Barclay Arms Hotel. Hoswick was a most important centre of the herring fishing industry but has adapted very well to the change in circumstances.

From the track to the beach take the well-constructed footbridge over the burn, which once served the burnt mound at Swinister, and head east by crossing a fence. Between Cullister and Stove are Sandwick Junior High School and the Swimming Pool. A series of helpful stiles lie on the route round the banks to Cumlewick and Broonies Taing. Here are signs of industrial activity both ancient (herring station) and modern but there would appear to be little future for the jetty and

warehouses of the oil supply base, the hopes for which have never been realised. On approaching the site follow a well-defined track up to a large wooden gate. Walk in front of the large warehouses, all rather eerie, and follow a track, which heads in direction of the sandy beach of Cumlewick. On the east side of the beach is a grass embankment once protected by a now decayed concrete sea wall and collapsed concrete access steps. All once part of the time when Herring Geos was aptly named. Cumlewick Ness has a geo through which the sea has made an access tunnel under the cliffs to form a passage cave. Some 30ft from the cliff edge the roof of the cave has collapsed and created the hole of The Kirn. It must have been quite a threat to livestock and walkers before being fenced off in a wire enclosure. It looks pretty evil from the top. There is indeed a local legend that a ship was once wrecked on The Ness one foggy night. The surviving sailors linked hands to walk up the banks but some were lost down the kirn.

No Ness comes into view, east as we round Cumlewick Ness and head past the deep geo, with cave, of Punds Ness. Climb up the slopes to two square planticrubs, one in a good state of repair the other barely existing. Struggle over a double wire fence to heathery slopes on which one can find a 5ft high flat stone cairn by some depressions in the ground. Higher up is another cairn, 3ft high by more depressions with flat stones in them. Descend to pass a jumble of assorted croft buildings and reach the road. The sandy beach of Sand Wick gives this large village its name.

Behind it stands the Sandwick Parish church, 1807 (St. Magnus) and the cemetery where a special stone enclosure segregates the Bruce family of Sand Lodge, Sumburgh and Lunna. Sandwick is a very active community and there are a variety of sporting and social clubs. The definitive guide to the area, 'Footsteps Through Sandwick', was created by members of Sandwick Youth and Community Centre in 1995. The book gives one all the information necessary to appreciate Sandwick and its environs. It also tells that every Sandwick man has a nickname so you could try finding that out if you meet a local on the banks!

Broonies' Taing in its prime as a fishing station. J. D. Rattar (circa 1925)

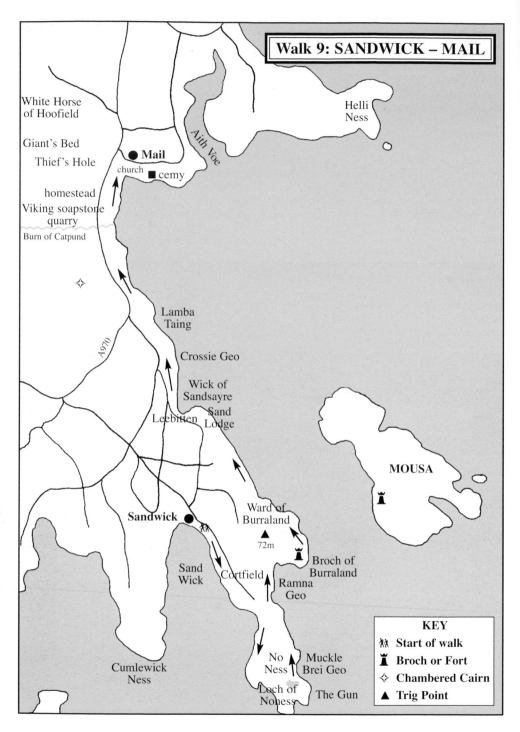

Walk 9: SANDWICK – MAIL

White Horse of Hoofield

Helli Ness

Giant's Bed

Thief's Hole

Aith Voe

● **Mail**

church ■ cemy

homestead

Viking soapstone quarry

Burn of Catpund

A970

Lamba Taing

Crossie Geo

Wick of Sandsayre

Sand Lodge

Leebitten

MOUSA

Sandwick ●

Ward of Burraland

▲ 72m

Broch of Burraland

Sand Wick

Cortfield

Ramna Geo

Cumlewick Ness

No Ness

Muckle Brei Geo

Loch of Noness

The Gun

KEY

🚶 **Start of walk**

♜ **Broch or Fort**

✧ **Chambered Cairn**

▲ **Trig Point**

WALK 9: SANDWICK – MAIL

7 miles (11 kms) : 4 hours

OS Maps: **Landranger Sheet 4 Shetland – South Mainland**
                 Pathfinder Sheet 32 Sandwick

A most interesting promontory, No Ness, takes up most of this walk allowing easy walking and highlights including the deserted area of Burraland and its impressive broch remains. Expect sailing activity in season at Sandsayre and end the walk under the watchful eye of the White Horse of Hoo Field.

Leave Sandwick by the road which heads south east towards No Ness. There are caves between Skerries of Curefield and Point of Rugg where there is a small geo with a boat winch in it. At No Ness a traditional water well has been restored and all is well tended, make for a stile adjacent to a gate and pass through some ornamental gate posts to reach an area of spoil

heaps and a concrete lined well. The cliffs remain low level but the ravages of the weather have helped shape an inshore stack into the shape of an elephant. Near the point of the Ness a slanted cave named Bannock Hole can be seen in its western bank, then pass the Stack of Billyageo and The Gun. Here is an octagonal concrete base and presumably near here is the site of a beacon light, which acted as a guide to shipping between 1887 and the 1950s. The Ness was notorious for shipwrecks.

The cliffs are now precipitous and crumbly so walk the Loch of No Ness and admire the birdlife bathing there. From Muckle Brei Geo four helpful stiles take one onto an area of

Sandwick – Sand Lodge and Mousa.

Catpund soapstone quarry.

Head north along the cliffs enjoying the views of Mousa, in the summer the P&O ferries sometimes glide through Mousa Sound on their way south. Before reaching the 17th century mansion of Sand Lodge, home of the Bruce family, we pass the remains of a copper mine. The shaft is now sealed where copper and iron ores were mined between 1789 and the early 1920s.

In front of the entrance of Sand Lodge note pedestal sundial (1789) and dovecot as we pass the impressive walled garden and so arrive at the Wick of Sandsayre, the main local base for sailing and where the annual Sandwick Regatta is held.

Leebotten pier is the place to catch the ferry to Mousa (see circular walk no. I) and the adjacent shingle beach was once used for salting and drying fish. Note the rows of miners cottages in the side of the hill above built as homes of the men who worked at the copper mine. It is not easy walking between the road and the cliff edge so use the road as necessary. A sealed shaft in the cliffs below Setter was the site of another, smaller, copper mine.

After Crossie Geo keep the option open of crossing the road and visiting a chambered cairn and then, at Burn of Catpund, a Norse soapstone (steatite) quarry. Part of the bedrock has been excavated and hollows left by the extraction of soapstone bowls can be seen as well as medieval quarrying scars. An interpretative display board helpfully explains this protected site.

A little further on at the edge of the cultivable land are two Neolithic homestead sites within an enclosure and Thief's Hole, the bolt hole for a North Mavine sheep thief named Kail Hulter who finally overstepped the mark and kidnapped a boy to work for him. Fortunately the boy outwitted him eventually and Kail Hulter was caught and hanged. The Giant's Bed near Vestinore I have yet to discover; at this point cross the extremely busy road to reach Mail. You are now viewed from the hill above by the White Horse of Hoofield.

The song about him goes like this …

several geos one of which has a beach with various stone ruins on it including a standing stone surrounded by rubble. Inshore seals enjoy basking on the flat rocks whilst offshore porpoises may be seen fishing.

East of Ramna Geo brings us to the western shore of the Sound of Mousa, at the foot of the Ward of Burraland where, almost directly opposite to the Broch of Mousa, is the broch of Burraland. Its location is in a position of great natural strength as it stands on the inner end of a high rocky promontory named Hoga. An iron age settlement site is immediately to its south. Although the broch is in a ruined state it is still standing to a height of 12ft in places. The location makes it one of the most appealing picnic spots in Shetland. The extensive croft ruins beyond the broch once formed the crofting community of Burland; in 1851 43 people lived in Burland but by 1893 only one person, Kitty Smith, lived there.

DA WHITE HORSE O' HOOFIELD

Ia da face ia auld Hoofield, high up ia da hill,
A muckle white horse staands sae pacefull an
still.
He's been traw da ages fae life first began
An he's niffer hed coarn ir ryegress ir bran.
He's niffer been yokit, he's niffer been shod
An he's niffer set fit pae da hard staenney rod.
He's niffer seen helter, stake, teddir ir swill,
He just staands by himsell ia da face ia da hill.

If da white horse ia Hoofield a story cud tell
He wid mind a da things at he's seen fur himsell.
He wid mind Mousa Castle being beelt lang ago
An da Picts kerryin stanes fae da banks doon
below.
He wid mind Julius Ceasar we ships comin nort
Fou dae rawed an dae sailed till dae wun into
port.
He wid mind da Norse Galleys we oars oot da
side
As dae rawed troo da soond agenst stormy wind
an tide.

He wid mind whin da Press Gang wis taking wir
men
An a lot o'dem niffer saw Shetland agen.
He wid mind da Dutch smugglers sail in tae da
weeks
An da men we dir clugs an dir wide baggy
breeks.
He wid mind men rawin off fur tobacco an gin

An da revenue cutter aft making dem rin.
He's seen boats becalmed oot be aest Grunnie
Baa
We gret shots ia herring wirt naethin awa.

He's seen boanny simmers and hard winters tue
An he's seen hugs an gimmers bein caaed ta da
crue,
Fok yallin, dugs barkin heard a aver da hill.
But da muckle white horse he just always stuid
still.
He's seen mony a pitprop an batten an dale
Comin in by da skerries tae land up at Mail.
He's seen mony a war brak fae warbrackin
carts
An da fok gaain we war athin kishies an kerts.

Da aest side o'Hoofield is rocky an' steep
We no muckle green pick fur kye in fur sheep
But da while horse just stands dere we niffer a
care
If da face o'auld Hoofield be barren ir bare.
An whin winter comes we da frost an da snaw
Da white horse o'Hoofield feels nae cauld awa
Cus he's no lek a horse we bluid, flesh, skin an
bane
Fur neture designed dat white horse oot ia
stane.

Eddie Smith

This song goes well to the tune:
"The Mountains of Mourne"

45

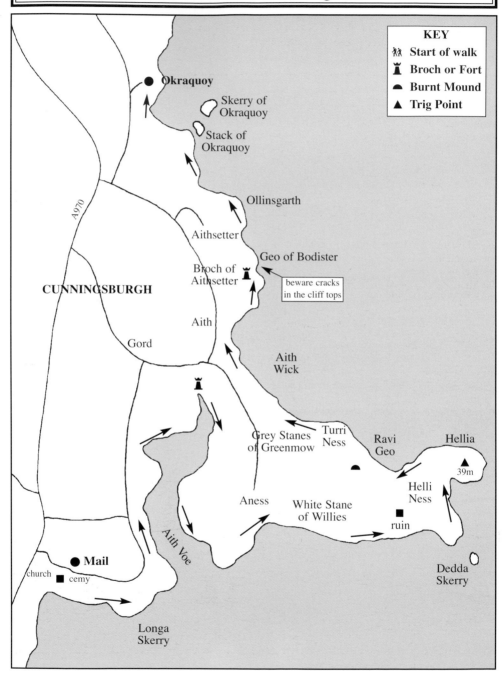

KEY
- 🏃 Start of walk
- ♜ Broch or Fort
- ⬮ Burnt Mound
- ▲ Trig Point

Okraquoy

Skerry of Okraquoy

Stack of Okraquoy

Ollinsgarth

A970

Aithsetter

Geo of Bodister

Broch of Aithsetter

beware cracks in the cliff tops

CUNNINGSBURGH

Aith

Gord

Aith Wick

Grey Stanes of Greenmow

Turri Ness

Ravi Geo

Hellia

39m

Helli Ness

Aness

White Stane of Willies

ruin

Dedda Skerry

Aith Voe

Mail

church ■ cemy

Longa Skerry

WALK 10: MAIL – OCRAQUOY

7 miles (11 kms) : 4 hours

OS Maps: **Landranger Sheet 4 Shetland – South Mainland**
Pathfinder Sheets 32 Sandwick
33 Scalloway

The area round Cunningsburgh ("The King's Fort") is a popular place to live and one of the main attractions must be Aith Voe round which this walk goes. The heathery slopes of Helli Ness are a contrast to the voe and between the Ness and Okraquoy are many delightful geos and one recognised broch site.

The distinctive former Manse of Mail stands beside the church and nearby cemetery where stands the war memorial to those lost in two World Wars. In 1992 a Pictish carved stone was found in the graveyard which shows a dog-headed man carrying an axe. It is on display in the Shetland Museum, Lerwick. Close to the church a rock 60ft from the shore and accessible at low water was once considered to be a broch site. A small conical stone recovered from it is now in the National Museum. Of the medieval chapel nothing

remains but at various times fragments of stones inscribed with oghams or runes have been found in this area including the stone illustrated, found at a depth of 3ft below the bed of a stream.

Aith Voe provides a marina and slipway and berthing points for the many boat owners and is probably the most sheltered haven on the east coast of Shetland south of Lerwick. The biggest danger to boats is the baa, the submerged rocks which are situated at the entrance to the voe and which are submerged in rough weather. Hay & Co. commenced fish curing operations here in 1844 and closed them in 1872. At the head of the Voe is a large mound, possibly a grass-covered broch. Walk south on to Aness, where I admired a fine selection of sunflowers blooming, and cross green grazing land to the slanting cliffs. To the

Tattie houses at Mail, possibly about 1900.

FIG. 470.—Stone with runic inscription from Mail, Cunningsburgh (No. 1136, 5).

[By Courtesy of the Society of Antiquaries of Scotland.]

Stone with ruin inscription from Mail.

north near the top of the slope of the hill is a prominent white boulder known as White Stane of Willies. There are several fences to be crossed going east along the Ward of Greenmow until a well built stone wall is reached. Beyond it is a semi-enclosed area where the walls have been constructed to allow the passage of air through them. The flat rocky shore is popular with basking seals as we turn southeast towards Holm of Helliness. The Holm is very green, as no sheep appear to cross the narrow but turbulent channel. Dedda Skerry is at its point.

There appears to be some sort of prehistoric settlement site on the small beach at Taing of Helliness, where on 6th January 1786 the

'Concordia' was wrecked, from which climb the hill alongside a wall to reach the prominent ruin. The house must have looked very splendid in its day and one can appreciate the dressed stone lintels, stone arch and large chimneybreast still surviving. It is all that remains of an old farmhouse associated with the Heddell family. The land at Helliness was once owned by Bergen Cathedral and by the Bruce family of Sumburgh. It was bought by Francis Heddell in 1827 and according to the 1855 census 28 people – farmers' and servants' families lived at Helliness. From here climb up to the Trig. Pt. (39m) and enjoy the excellent views from it.

Descend past sheer sided Uxna Geo and

Cunningsburgh Marina.

48

distinctive stack of Hellia to walk the northern shore where a burnt mound will be found in a small geo beside a burn. There are many planti-crubs on the sheltered slopes and when a ruined croft is reached climb up to the right of it, across marshy ground where a flat raised stone enclosure will be seen. Dominating the skyline are the Grey Stanes of Greenmow, one huge boulder 200 yds to the east of two smaller ones. On the approach to the houses at Aith old boat noosts in the cliffs will be seen. The cliff path is quite narrow. A helpful stile takes one over a fence near the horizontal cleft of Longi Geo; cross a burn and so arrive at the broch of Aithsetter.

The remains of this broch are situated on a high rocky promontory known as Blogars-hellia and are completely overgrown with turf. The headland is linked to the mainland by a narrow neck, across which there are still some traces of defensive works. There is quite a large hollow in the centre in which one can stand and survey some of the area.

From the broch head north for Geo of Bodista taking care to avoid some evil cracks in the cliff

Cunningsburgh – Grey Stanes, Greenmow.

tops. It is then a stiff climb up to Ollinsgarth from which there is a good view of the broch, now below. The Skerry and the Stack of Okraquoy – two large areas of flat black rocks just offshore – are now in view. Descend towards the Bay of Okraquoy passing a derelict croft and planti-crub. A burn running through a deep cleft to the sea has to be negotiated.

This accomplished, cross another burn and so reach Bay of Okraquoy where boats may be found drawn up on the large pebbly beach.

Broch at Aithsetter.

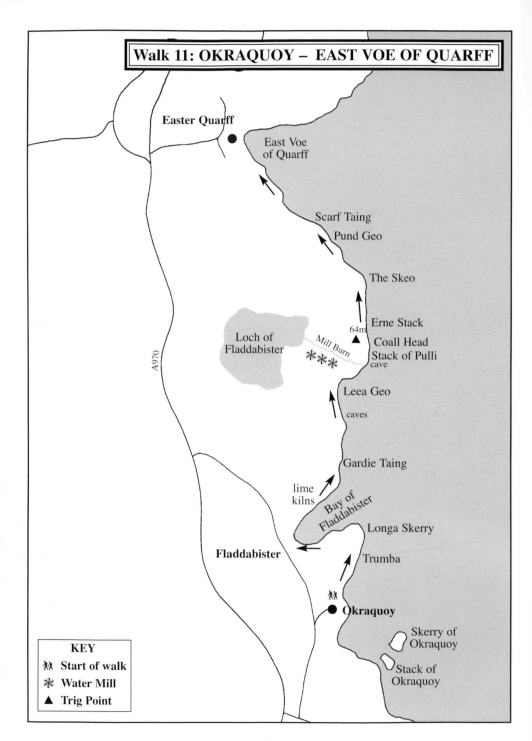

Walk 11: OKRAQUOY – EAST VOE OF QUARFF

Easter Quarff

East Voe
of Quarff

Scarf Taing

Pund Geo

The Skeo

Erne Stack

64m

Coall Head

Stack of Pulli

cave

Loch of
Fladdabister

Mill Burn

Leea Geo

caves

A970

Gardie Taing

lime
kilns

Bay of
Fladdabister

Longa Skerry

Fladdabister

Trumba

Okraquoy

Skerry of
Okraquoy

Stack of
Okraquoy

KEY

🚶 **Start of walk**

✳ **Water Mill**

▲ **Trig Point**

WALK 11: OKRAQUOY – EAST VOE OF QUARFF

3 miles (5 kms) : 2 hours

OS Maps: **Landranger Sheet 4 Shetland – South Mainland**
Pathfinder Sheet 33 Scalloway

This lovely walk includes the coastal area of Fladdabister where a band of crystalline limestone runs across the countryside increasing the fertility of the soil and the variety of wild flowers. The ruined limekilns are now a romantic feature. Superb variety of caves to be seen in the rugged cliffs. Exercise caution on cliff tops.

We leave the well protected crofting settlement round Okraquoy by heading north and climbing up the small cliffs of Trumba. Descend over a stile to the low-level banks beside a rocky shore. The view up the coast is dominated by Coall Head.   Another stile has been thoughtfully built to help one negotiate a field

drain. On the other side of the fence note an area of stone clearance cairns tucked into a fold in the hill. Offshore the jagged edge of Longa Skerry curves northeast.

The access to Fladdabister Bay, which is often ablaze with wild flowers, is made easier because there are stoutly constructed stiles over which one passes, below a cairn on a knoll, to cross a burn. A small cove is popular with seals and above it rise the crags upon which stand the ruins of two lime kilns. In these beehive kilns limestone and peat were burned together to produce lime for buildings and agricultural purposes. Super views from these ruins. The kilns were in use until the 1930s.

Lime kilns, Fladdabister, and Bressay.

Peat and lime were placed in alternate layers, rising two feet or more above the top of the kiln. The peat would be lit and once fired the kiln would burn for hours. Eventually water would be poured onto the hot limestone to convert it into white lime. Some of the lime would be taken to the beach in Bay of Fladdabister and then taken by boat to Lerwick. There are the ruins of another lime kiln at Glover. Further round the bay is a small wired off enclosure before a fence over which one climbs to enter a jungle area of assorted plant life including masses of lilies. Climb upon to Gardie Taing, a rocky headland on the south flank of which is a natural dolmen – like arrangement of boulders. Useful stiles help one round the next small geo and burn where I enjoyed the sight of a large flock of twite twittering as they sat on the wire fence.

The next stretch of cliff is extremely dramatic for there are assorted stacks close onshore and the cliffs feature vertical fissured cracks and caves. Beware the cliff edges as it is quire confusing as to which is the mainland and which are grass covered stacks, such as Pulli, beckoning one on. We can now view the deep caves of Coall Head but it is the variety of caves in the cliffs of Leea Geo, which first attract our close interest. This geo features one of the most impressive collection of caves that I have ever seen.

Now make for the Trig. Pt. topped peak of Coall Head, keeping well in from the cliff edge. Unfortunately we have to lose ground before regaining it once having crossed a small valley through which a burn runs. This is the boisterous Burn of Fladdabister, which tumbles down from the Loch of Fladdabister. I wish I could have seen it when its strength was harnessed to power several water mills, the ruins of which can be seen upstream nearer the loch.

The view from the Trig. Pt. (64m) of Coall Head is one of the delights of this walk and it requires effort to leave it and descend its natural ramparts to the cliffs. We pass a striking conical stack inshore and The Skeo (no sign of any ruined fish curing building) and Scarf Taing (plenty of signs of them!) to enter East Voe of Quarff. It is unrestricted easy tramping to reach the croft at the head of the voe, passing small geos, which usually have a quota of seals. A large heap of boulders border a pebbly beach, which provides a haven for small fishing boats, based at Quarff.

WALK 12: EAST VOE OF QUARFF – GULBERWICK

3 miles (5 kms) : 2 hours

OS Maps: **Landranger Sheet 4 Shetland – South Mainland**
Pathfinder Sheet 33 Scalloway

Another Broch of Burland to be explored and other sites of ancient habitation – all in contrast to thriving Gulberwick which has proved increasingly popular with people who wish to be both near Lerwick and untouched open country.

From the beach of Easter Quarff head north to cross a burn which flows down to the bay past a redundant church standing east of the main road. Climb onto the bluff of small rounded hills and walk down to the shore and a boulder-strewn cove. The island of Bressay dominates the view east as we cross a fence by Longa Geo, where the cliff formations is like a serrated rock pavement.

Ascend the Gards where a large boulder has the foundation of a cairn being built upon it. From here is a superb view of the south side of Broch of Burland perched on the cliff opposite. To get to it walk down to a burn and follow it west to a wooden bridge. Up the valley the quarry and crofts of Brindister stand out on the high ground. Brindister is a place of ancient settlement; a burnt mound site is to be found here and on the Loch of Brindister are the remains of a fortification, a Dun, on a small islet. There is no evidence of any causeway connecting it with the shore. Cross the bridge and walk up to a solid croft ruin and from the cliff edge view seals lying up on the flat rocks below. I risked life and limb to pick some

Broch of Burland (Brindister).

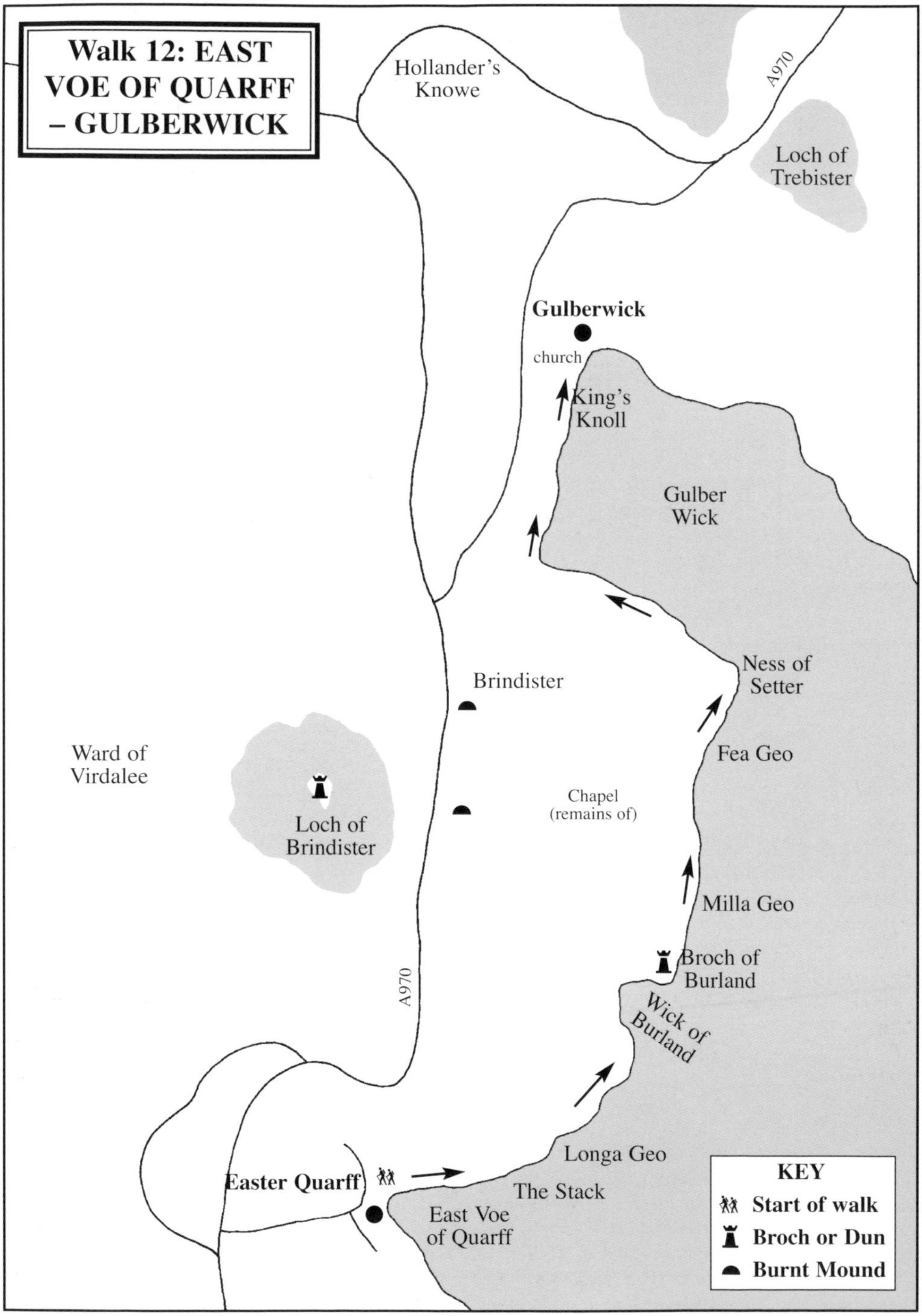
Walk 12: EAST VOE OF QUARFF – GULBERWICK
Hollander's Knowe
A970
Loch of Trebister
Gulberwick
church
King's Knoll
Gulber Wick
Ness of Setter
Brindister
Fea Geo
Ward of Virdalee
Chapel (remains of)
Loch of Brindister
Milla Geo
Broch of Burland
A970
Wick of Burland
Longa Geo
Easter Quarff
The Stack
East Voe of Quarff
KEY
Start of walk
Broch or Dun
Burnt Mound

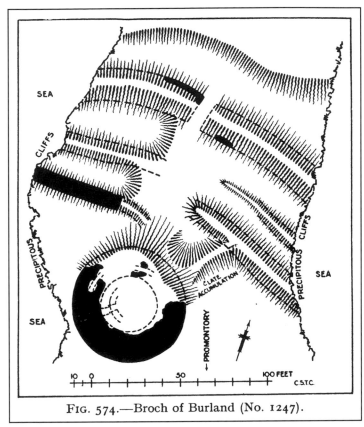

FIG. 574.—Broch of Burland (No. 1247).

Broch of Burland (Brindister) – plan.

delicious field mushrooms here watched all the while by nervous seals below! Climb to Broch of Burland where three ramparts and ruin of the broch itself are most impressive; the site is protected on three sides by precipitous cliffs while approach to it from the north is barred by the formidable series of defensive ditches and ramparts. Despite it being a ruin it is not difficult to imagine how noble it must have looked.

Leave the broch and climb up the cliffs keeping well inland, as they are precipitous here. It is better to climb higher then follow the sheep track along the cliff edge between Milla Geo and Fea Geo, where there is a natural arch in the making. The rocky mound at Ness of Setter broods over flat skerries popular with flocks of shags. Gulber Wick is now in view and we

walk the southern shore, over two burns and a wire fence, to an ancient shore enclosure in the boundary of the township. Many smart dwelling houses have transformed this bay in recent years. At the head of the bay pass through a stone wall and explore the turf-covered mound. This is the 'King's Knoll' but its origins are unknown. Walk through some rough uncultivated ground towards the small sandy beach at the road end below the school and kirk and go through a metal kissing gate to reach the beach.

The Orkneying saga records that the Norse Earl Rognvald was shipwrecked in GulberWick in 1148. Centuries later a silver penannular Viking brooch was found here (now in the Shetland Museum) so the place does have royal connections.

WALK 13: GULBERWICK – SOUND

3½ miles (5.6 kms) : 2 hours

OS Maps: **Landranger Sheet 4 Shetland – South Mainland**
Pathfinder Sheet 33 Scalloway

An interesting walk around Ness of Trebister where green grazing land gives way to rough heather. Plenty of seals and seabirds to spot on the way.

Leave the beach at Gulberwick and climb onto the low-level banks below the large croft at Trebister. On the banks is a decayed boat winch whilst by the water a rusting hoist. No boat activity manifest in this area now. The walls of the burial ground are in the cliff edge so go over a field gate and go round past its gate. Cross two field gates to reach the burn at Stava Geo and cross it where it passes a ruined

water mill. The Ness of Trebister gets more interesting the further one is along it and at Tinda note a natural arch. The point has a green plateau and is dominated by Punds stack. The view down the deep geo takes in the sharp north headland of Mousa far south on the horizon.

Opposite the Bressay lighthouse turn into the Voe of Sound at The Nizz. Rafts of guillemots may be spotted in the water here. Lerwick comes increasingly into view with the Town Hall dominant on the horizon, a magnificent landmark and building which celebrated its

Tresbister, Gulberwick, mill ruin.

56

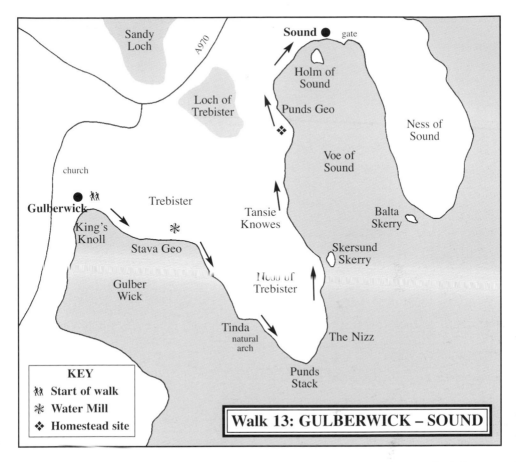

Walk 13: GULBERWICK – SOUND

KEY
🚶🚶 Start of walk
❋ Water Mill
❖ Homestead site

Map labels:
Sandy Loch
A970
Sound · gate
Holm of Sound
Loch of Trebister
Punds Geo
Ness of Sound
Voe of Sound
church
Gulberwick
Trebister
Tansie Knowes
Balta Skerry
King's Knoll
Stava Geo
Skersund Skerry
Gulber Wick
Head of Trebister
Tinda
natural arch
The Nizz
Punds Stack

centenary in August 1983. The slopes of Tansie Knowes provide a study in contrast for the wild moorland scene seems odd against the urban backdrop. Seals find great lie up places on Skersund Skerry, as do shags. It is quite tough tramping through the heather but it gets easier once the ancient homestead site between the Loch of Trebister and the sheep fold ruin at Punds Geo is reached. Planticrubs have been built on the side of the hill and I found two pairs of wheatears prepared to lead the way along and over a wire fence. We reach a pebbly beach where rust two old boat winches and cross a burn below the walled burial ground. A footpath leads left to a stile and access to Upper Sound. Our path continues up the slope above the shore to a wooden kissing gate above a sandy beach. From here is access to Kantersted Road and thence Sound Service Centre and Clickimin Broch.

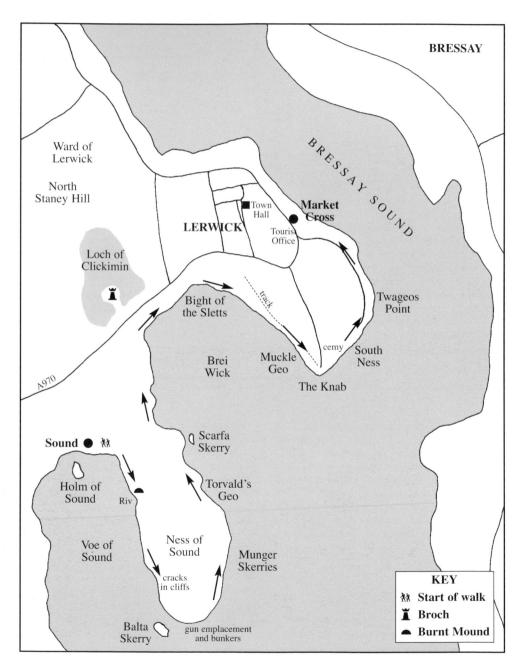

BRESSAY

Ward of
Lerwick

North
Staney Hill

B R E S S A Y   S O U N D

Town Hall

Market Cross

LERWICK

Tourist Office

Loch of
Clickimin

track

Bight of
the Sletts

Twageos
Point

Brei
Wick

Muckle
Geo

cemy

South
Ness

A970

The Knab

Sound

Scarfa
Skerry

Holm of
Sound

Riv

Torvald's
Geo

Voe of
Sound

Ness of
Sound

Munger
Skerries

cracks
in cliffs

Balta
Skerry

gun emplacement
and bunkers

KEY

Start of walk

Broch

Burnt Mound

WALK 14: SOUND – LERWICK MARKET CROSS

4 miles (7.5 kms) : 2 hours

OS Maps: **Landranger Sheet 4 Shetland – South Mainland**
Pathfinder Sheet 33 Sandwick
44 Lerwick

The final stretch of the South Mainland walk is full of interest and extra time should be allowed if Clickimin Broch is going to be visited as part of this walk. Great views of Bressay and Lerwick and good for wildlife especially ducks and geese. Take care on the cliffs at the point of the Ness.

We continue north round Ness of Sound by crossing the sand and shingle beach and making for grazing land and a burnt mound on its western banks. Seafield House and the farm stand out towards the south of the Ness. The sight of Bard Head on Bressay gives warning of the approaching end of the Ness. The cliffs are quite deceptive so climb well inland up and over a grey rocky escarpment where there are also various cracks and fissures to be avoided. On top of the escarpment are various sections of concrete hardstanding once used to site signal masts on. Walk down to a fence facing Bressay and follow it to an area of World War 2 gun emplacements and bunkers; one is particularly perilously perched on the cliffs now. Enjoy views of Lerwick before walking slightly inland to avoid three small geos. Circuit a decayed storage tank area at the end of its fence where it approaches a stone wall. There is just room to squeeze through and gain access to a tarmac road at a turning point. On a small houb you may find ducks (mainly mallard) and geese enjoying the miniature lake. The road continues through the houses to the South Lochside junction roundabout near Clickimin Broch. The broch should be visited; access is by pathway and an interpretive sign explains that the promontory in the loch, on which the broch ruin stands, was inhabited approximately from 100BC to AD500, "over 15 centuries it was extensively built over and rebuilt. It was

Clickimin and Ness of Sound from Staney Hill.

59

Clickimin Broch and leisure centre.

partially 'restored' in the 1850s. Further excavation and restoration in the 1950s produced the site's present appearance".

Return to South Lochside junction and take the pavement on the right hand side of road until just before the rather appealing first house on the right. Follow a route sign, "The Sletts 1/3' through a kissing gate and follow the tarmac path along the shoreline, which features large flat rocks.

Concrete steps descend to an old slipway but our path continues to a kissing gate and we turn right up Breiwick Road. On the right hand side just after passing a stone wall is a walking route sign, "The Knab 1/3". Walk up the path between lush grassy slopes and the shoreline popular with oyster catchers and stacks topped by shags. Shore activity can best be viewed through a strategically placed gap in the wall. Climb up to a gate and a road-end turning circle and take a walking route sign, "Twageos ¼". On the shoreline World War II defence sites can be seen and just before and below South Ness House, the first house on the right of the road, are two pill boxes and a navigation light.

From South Ness House walk down Twageos Road noting the Arthur Anderson Homes for Widows which the MP for Orkney and Shetland and Chairman of P&O built in memory of his wife. Also on the right is a domestic garage roofed with a boat. Commercial Street takes one past such landmarks as the Lerwick Boating Club, the Lodberries, Charlotte House and the Queens Hotel. Turn right down to the harbour area and opposite Victoria Pier the Market Cross will be found standing in front of the Tourist Information Centre. The Cross fittingly marks the end of the South Mainland walk and there is now the opportunity to explore bustling Lerwick and its many attractions.

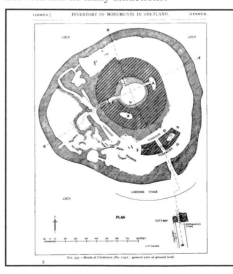

Broch of Clickimin – plan.

CIRCULAR WALK A

ST. NINIAN'S ISLE
3.5 miles (5.6 kms) : 2 hours

OS Maps: **Landranger Sheet 4 Shetland – South Mainland**
                    Pathfinder Sheet 32 Sandwick

Bigton and Ireland lie in a fertile area of Mainland Shetland between the hills to the east and glorious sea views to the west. The skyline west is dominated, at a distance, by Foula. In the foreground and easily accessible is St. Ninian's Isle, which contains the ruins of a 12th Century church and a holy well. A magnificent shell-sand tombolo links the island to the mainland. A truly memorable walk.

Start the walk at the shop/Post Office in the centre of Bigton. Public toilets are also conveniently situated near here. Admire attractive gardens and well-manicured lawns before following sign-posted track down to a car park. Note the impressive mansion, the Haa of Bigton, on the southern edge of the village. An interpretive display board at the car park gives some information about the tombolo, the island and the excavations which lead to the discovery of the 'St Ninian's Isle Treasure' in 1958. The tombolo is a strand of sand between Bigton Wick and St. Ninian's Bay and crossing it can normally be accomplished without wetting your feet but be prepared to get them wet in certain high tide conditions. The bay is popular with eider ducks and wagtails.

Climb the sandbanks of the island and turn north to reach the enclosed remains of the church which, like the island, was dedicated to St. Ninian. St. Ninian was a 5th century Celtic saint whose activities were pastoral and monastic rather than missionary. According to Bede he converted the Southern Picts. A revival of the cult of St. Ninian took place in the 12th century and he is commemorated in almost every county in of Scotland.

St. Ninian's Isle – church. Ireland and Bigton in the background.

The most exciting find of Shetland archeology was made by Douglas Coutts, a onetime colleague of mine at Sullom Voe Terminal, when he was a 15 year old schoolboy in 1958 assisting Dr Andrew O'Dell of Aberdeen University.

Douglas, within three hours of digging away with his trowel, discovered a hoard of Celtic silverware, which has been hailed as "the biggest find of its kind in Scotland". Douglas had joined the 12-strong team during the summer holidays after attending a public lecture in Lerwick by Professor O'Dell. "Having heard what Professor O'Dell had to say about his work on the St. Ninian's isle dig it fired my curiosity," Douglas told 'Sullom Voe Scene' many years later. "After he had given his address he asked for volunteers to help his dozen or so students in their excavations. I was the only person present who put himself forward. When I got to the site, the whole of the interior floor of the old church had been excavated to bedrock. I started digging away on one part of the site when I got down to a stone slab which was marked with a Celtic cross."

"Beneath this stone was box, approximately one foot square, which contained the collection of silverware which has been dated back to 800 AD. The cache included 12 brooches of Celtic design, many inset with semi-precious stones, numerous bowls and a hanging lamp and other objects".

The collection is now in the Royal Museum in Queen Street, Edinburgh although replicas of some of the larger items can be viewed in the Shetland Museum, Lerwick.

From the church ruins head north for Loose Head. It is a gentle climb with distant views of the majestic red cliffs of Westerwick hopefully blazing in reflected sun. One dilapidated stone wall has to be crossed before reaching the Trig. Pt. on Loose Head. One can walk further but it is risky and the view of the impressive stack off the head is best enjoyed from Ireland. Return down the western bank where the black sheets

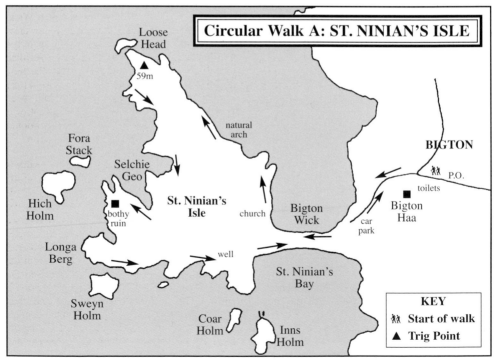

St. Ninian's Isle – Holy Well.

of rock containing a natural arch slope down to the sea. Be prepared for Bonxie attacks in summer. Round Selchie Geo and climb onto the promontory opposite Hich Holm where a ruined bothy can at least provide a wind break. From Longa Berg onwards the view south is dominated by the smaller islands, which cluster round St. Ninian, Sweyn, Coar and Inns all providing grazing for sheep.

Make for the main track, which goes down to the tombolo. There is a well-preserved stone wall with a gate. Go through this and find St. Ninian's well in a marshy area about 200 yards south of the track.

Return across the tombolo and climb the track back into Bigton.

Robert Leask, a Bigton authority, recounts two unusual tales about events on St. Ninian's Isle.

In 1822 the smuggler's sloop "Earl Spencer" was wrecked in Shingley Geo. All the crew were saved apart from one and he was buried in the kirkyard. However, Bigton folk noted that no treasure had been salvaged or, if it had, it had been hidden somewhere. The secret location of this other St. Ninian's Isle treasure was not discovered until three years later when a schooner was spotted at anchor in North Wick. The schooner launched a boat and her crew were to be seen on the isle and digging in the graveyard. Later a black chest was unearthed and transported back to the ship. By the time the Bigton men reached the isle they could only observe that the smuggler's grave had been opened and that the imprint of a chest was visible on the sandy soil. The schooner meantime had sailed west over the horizon.

It was also in the kirkyard that the crofter's champion Jeemie Sinclair of Brake had a 'gluff' (surprise). One Christmas he went to St. Ninian's Isle to hunt rabbits but as he approached the kirkyard he was horrified to see a coffin rise up and tilted at one end, move slowly towards him. Jeemie stood his ground, armed as he was with a gun salvaged from the ship 'Atlas', wrecked in 1807. He raised the gun and commanded, "Not a step closer or I'll fire". The coffin slowed, halted and then retreated with increasing speed. It was Jeemie's brother Robbie who later confessed to being the man in the coffin and who in the event had suffered more fright than he gave.

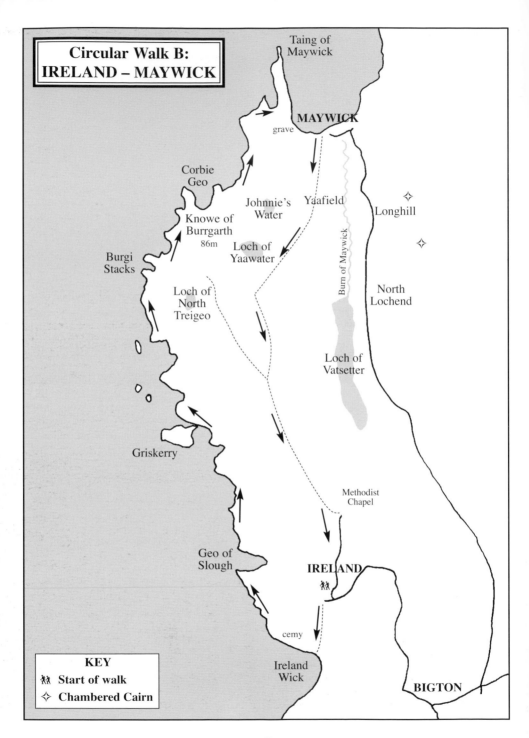

Circular Walk B:
IRELAND – MAYWICK

Taing of
Maywick

MAYWICK

grave

Corbie
Geo

Johnnie's
Water

Yaafield

Longhill

Knowe of
Burrgarth
86m

Loch of
Yaawater

Burgi
Stacks

Loch of
North
Treigeo

Burn of Maywick

North
Lochend

Loch of
Vatsetter

Griskerry

Methodist
Chapel

Geo of
Slough

IRELAND

cemy

Ireland
Wick

BIGTON

KEY
Start of walk
✧ **Chambered Cairn**

CIRCULAR WALK B

IRELAND – MAYWICK
5 miles (8 kms) : 2½ hours

OS Maps: **Landranger Sheet 4 Shetland – South Mainland**
Pathfinder Sheet HU 32/42 Sandwick

An enjoyable cliff walk with the option of returning either the way you have walked or returning by an inland route past the loch of Vatsetter or by walking south down the unclassified road.

From Ireland take the road which runs south from the village down to the beach at Ireland Wick. Walk northwest along a gated track, which goes to the walled cemetery. This is not thought to be the site of the 'Old Kirk'; a medieval round-towered church, one of the three in Shetland in the middle ages. The other two were built at Papil, Burra, and at Tingwall. Tradition tells that they were built by three sisters. The one on the Ness of Ireland (the actual site not known) probably fell into decay sometime in the 18th century. Brand saw it in 1701 but Low in 1774 found only some remains in existence. The tower of the churches could have been between 60-70 feet high and may have resembled one in Egilsay in Orkney.

There now begins a gradual climb, which takes one round the attractive Geo of Slough and up

Ness of Ireland at sunset.

to the cliff tops. Catch your breath by pausing to admire the stack of Griskerry. It is quite an impressive stretch of coastline from here round past Burgi Stacks reaching a high spot on the Knowe of Burgarth (86m) above Corbie Geo.

Walk down onto the Taing of Maywick from which are superb views of Clift Sound, the island of South Havra and Burra Isle. Maywick is a most attractive settlement, well protected from the south westerlys. One is reminded however of the cruelty of the sea by a poignant stone memorial set in the cliff edge in memory of a fisherman, Laurence Smith.

To return to Ireland follow the track up to Yaafield and to the top of the hill from which the whole of Loch of Vatsetter can be viewed below. Pick up a hill track, which goes down to Ireland and passes a Methodist Chapel.

Alternatively walk the road which heads south to the east of Loch of Vatsetter. The road route offers the opportunity of exploring two cairns, all that remains of prehistoric chambered tombs. The first is at 300 ft on the hillside east of Longhill and within it are seven stones set on edge. Two upright stones in the centre may be portal stones at the entry into a chamber. The site appears to represent a heel-shaped cairn later enlarged into a round cairn.

The second cairn is also at about 300 ft on the hillside east of North Lochend. It is made up of fairly large stones, now scattered round the immediate area.

Ireland and St. Ninian's Isle.

CIRCULAR WALK C

THE MOSQUITO MEMORIAL AT ROYL DALE
5 miles (8 kms) : 3 hours

OS Maps: **Landranger Sheet 4 Shetland – South Mainland**
             Pathfinder Sheet HU 32/42 Sandwick

A cross country walk from the main road to the coast where a memorial to the crew of a World War II RAF Mosquito stands near surviving wreckage at the crash site. The walk can be extended by two miles by returning from Royl Dale via Hoo Field and the Viking soapstone quarries at Cat Pund.

South of the junction between A970 Lerwick-Sumburgh Road and the turning to Hoswick a former loop of the old road still remains on the north side of the new road. A track to the peat hill heads north from it. Walk up the track taking the left-hand track at the first junction. At the second junction take the right track until

it peters out at Burn of Hamarifield. The aim is now to head northeast dropping down the slopes of Hamari Field and making for a stout wire fence, which stretches, from east to west. Keep to the right of the fence, as it is less boggy and walk west. It is possible you may spot grouse and mountain hares on this area of moorland. Aim to arrive on a grassy plateau, which lies below the top of Royl Field above the cliffs. The granite memorial to the mosquito crew and parts of the aircraft will be found south of Royl Dale, at OS Grid Reference 392205.

On the memorial are inscribed the following words: 'This memorial commemorates de

A Mosquito engine with memorial, Royl Dale and author.

Circular Walk C: MOSQUITO MEMORIAL AT ROYL DALE

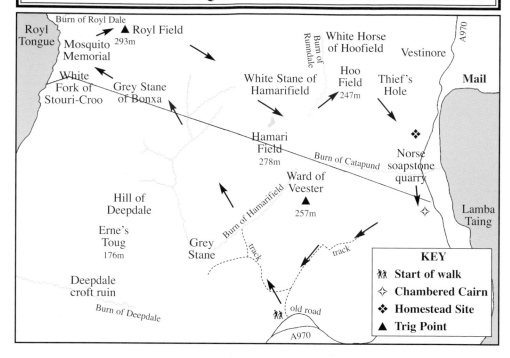

Royl Tongue

Burn of Royl Dale

▲ Royl Field
293m

Mosquito Memorial

White Fork of Stouri-Croo

Grey Stane of Bonxa

Burn of Runndale

White Horse of Hoofield

Vestinore

White Stane of Hamarifield

Hoo Field
247m

Thief's Hole

Mail

A970

Hamari Field
278m

Burn of Catapund

Norse soapstone quarry

Ward of Veester
▲ 257m

Hill of Deepdale

Erne's Toug
176m

Deepdale croft ruin

Burn of Deepdale

Burn of Hamarifield

Grey Stane

track

track

old road

Lamba Taing

A970

KEY

🏃🏃 **Start of walk**

✧ **Chambered Cairn**

❖ **Homestead Site**

▲ **Trig Point**

Mosquito memorial, Royl Dale. Burra Isle beyond.

Havilland Mosquito Mk VII "DZ642" of 627 Squadron Royal Air Force. Pilot – Flt Lt John A Reid RAF 48900 Navigator Fg Off Wesley D Irwin RCAF J16115. Returning from target marking on ill-fated raid on U-boat pens at Trondheim, Norway, short of fuel and in bad visibility the aircraft hit Royl Hill on 22nd November 1944 at 23.00 hours'.

The wreckage of the Mosquito and its crew was not discovered until 5th December when George Mann of Uphouse, Lawrence Malcolmson of Culbinsgarth and Robbie Jarmson of Cunningsburgh found it whilst they were out driving sheep. Years later Mark Reeder, a Bristow helicopter pilot noticed the crash site and began researching helped by an ex-627 navigator Andrew Denholm. Andrew came across John Mann whose uncle George was one of the men who found the wreckage and a watch. Shortly before he died George asked John to take the watch and try and trace a relative of the crew to give it to. Subsequently, nearly 50 years after the crash, the watch was presented to Wesley Irwin's widow Liley and his son Douglas. Douglas took the watch home and after placing it beside the bed that night he woke up to find his own watch had misted up and stopped! Mike Hopkins, on learning about the wreckage was surprised to find there was no memorial to the men who had died there. He researched the crash and funded this memorial which now fittingly marks the spot.

Return by the way you came or climb east to the summit of Royl Field, Trig. Pt. 293m, the highest hill (just) in South Mainland. The views can be spectacular.

From Royl Field descend, east, to cross the Burn of the Run and climb the north slope of Hamari Field. Cross the Burn of Russdale and climb to the top of Hoo Field 244m. Good views of Cunningsburgh and Mousa. The slopes of Hoo Field boast a Thief's Hole and two blocks of quartz rock one, on the south resembles a helicopter whilst the other, north, is known as The White Horse of Hoo Field. Walk down to Cat Pund where the Norse soapstone quarries will be found with an interpretive display board. Walk up the lower slopes of Ward of Veester passing a chambered cairn and link up with another peat track, which descends, south, to the start point of this walk.

Malcolm and Magnus Bray with a peat sledge near the Burn of Hamarifield.

CIRCULAR WALK D

SOUTH HAVRA
2½ miles (4 kms) : 2 hours

OS Maps: **Landranger Sheet 4 Shetland – South Mainland**
                          Pathfinder Sheet HU 32/42 Sandwick

South Havra is an uninhabited island today but was once home to a thriving little community which had its own school. It is easily spotted from afar because the remains of a windmill stands out as a dramatic landmark.

To reach the landing place make for a narrow entrance which widens to a shingle beach at the Harbour below North Ham. It gives immediate access to the area of South Havra once lived in. A shipwrecked crew are buried under the grassy slope of the side of the geo. Walk across rough grazing to the ruined windmill, which was built to grind meal in the 19th century. Evidently it was not a success. It is easy walking the coastline and from the north coast enjoys views of Houss Ness and Kettla Ness. At the Point of Skeo Geos look across to the island of Little Havra which boasts a cairn and some fine natural arches.

The north coast has caves and natural arches and it is easy walking all the way back to North Ham. Although the island had no fast running burn to power a water mill there was wind enough for a windmill, perhaps too much! Water was obtained from a well on the slopes below the windmill Trig. Pt. (42m).

Annie Deyell taught at the South Havra School 1917-1918 and tells of a population of 32 whilst she was there. Toddlers were tethered to prevent them falling over the banks. It was a difficult place to live and in 1923 the last of the Havra folk were leaving the island after 400 years of occupation. Mary Ann Jamieson, who now lives at Easter Hogaland on Burra Isle, was a pupil at the Havra School and remembers how happy life was on Havra and how sad it was to leave.

South and Little Havra from Hill of Deepdale.

70

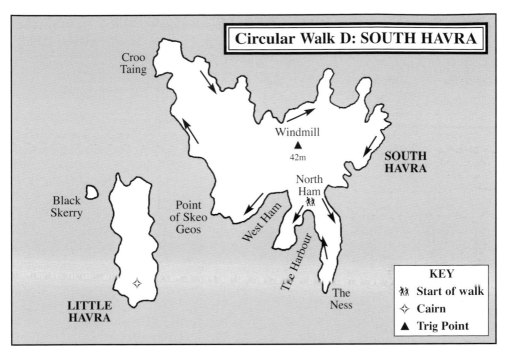

Circular Walk D: SOUTH HAVRA

Croo Taing

SOUTH HAVRA

Windmill
▲
42m

North Ham

Black Skerry

Point of Skeo Geos

West Ham

Tre Harbour

The Ness

LITTLE HAVRA

KEY
🕴 Start of walk
✧ Cairn
▲ Trig Point

South Havra – derelict windmill.

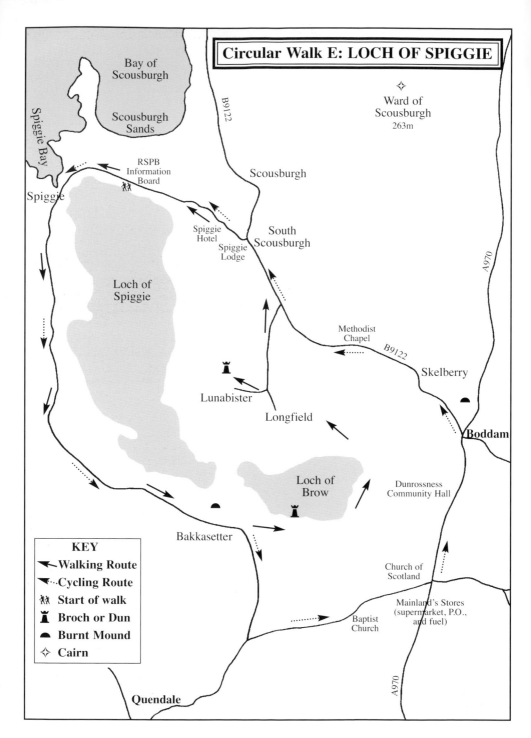

Circular Walk E: LOCH OF SPIGGIE

Bay of Scousburgh

Scousburgh Sands

Spiggie Bay

Spiggie

B9122

Ward of Scousburgh
263m

Scousburgh

RSPB Information Board

Spiggie Hotel

Spiggie Lodge

South Scousburgh

Loch of Spiggie

Methodist Chapel

B9122

Skelberry

A970

Lunabister

Longfield

Boddam

Loch of Brow

Dunrossness Community Hall

Bakkasetter

Church of Scotland

Mainland's Stores (supermarket, P.O., and fuel)

Baptist Church

A970

Quendale

KEY

- ← Walking Route
- ◄···· Cycling Route
- 👫 Start of walk
- ♟ Broch or Dun
- ⬛ Burnt Mound
- ✧ Cairn

72

CIRCULAR WALK E

LOCH OF SPIGGIE
5 miles (8 kms) : 2½ hours

OS Maps: **Landranger Sheet 4 Shetland – South Mainland**
Pathfinder Sheet HU 31/41 Sumburgh

This route is a favourite cycle run of mine but although largely a road walk it is equally enjoyable on foot and you may see even more!

The Loch of Spiggie is renowned for good trout fishing and with the Loch of Brow is an important Nature Reserve. In summer the lochs host wading birds and provide a bathing facility for arctic terns and skuas. In winter however it has attracted up to 400 whooper swans, gray lag geese, golden eye, wigeon, teal, pochard and up to 50 long tailed ducks. Enjoy a nature walk, mainly on quiet roads, which includes a prehistoric burnt mound site, a dun and a broch ruin.

Start from RSPB interpretive display board on the north shore of Loch of Spiggie and follow the road west. On our right are the Scousburgh Sands, a popular bathing and picnic beach. As the road swings south visit the small, romantic

Dun, Loch of Brow.

Spiggie bay, where there is a boathouse by some ancient noosts and slipway. It is one of Shetland's most photogenic spots for the red cliffs rise each side of the bay, from the middle of which is an excellent view up Muckle Sound of Foula on the far horizon. Return to the road and follow it to the south end of the loch. Here at Bakkasetter is a large concentric burnt mound standing in marshy ground.

Now make for Loch of Brow near the southern shore of which is a small islet with the remains of a small fort, a dun, on it. Little remains but it is thought that there was a passage of stepping stones and a roughly laid causeway which once connected it with the shore. Today a ruined planticrub dominates the islet and this is occupied by several pairs of fulmars who appear well prepared to defend their territory.

(1) If on foot splodge round Loch of Brow anti-clockwise and cross a footbridge before climbing up to Longfield and visiting the broch site at Lunabister. The ruin is a large grass covered mound in which traces of masonry have been exposed. During the construction of the house, Broch Cottage, on the edge of the mound masses of material as found in burnt

Beware! The broch on the Loch of Brow is today defended by a small army of fulmars.

Jennifer Nisbet

The Shetland Cycling Club at Spiggie Hotel, 1897. James Prophet Isbister

mounds was unearthed. A considerable number of relics were also uncovered including a trough-quern, a saddle-quern, many hammer stones and pounders, pieces of hard grained pottery and calcinated ox bones and ox teeth.

From Broch Cottage use its access road and follow it to join the main B9122 road leaving it at South Scousburgh to descend, west, past Spiggie Lodge and Spiggie Hotel and return to the start point.

(2) If cycling return to the road from Loch of Brow and climb up towards Quendale taking

Burnt mound, Skelberry.

the first junction, left, towards the A970. On the south of road pass the Baptist Chapel, with its distinctive castellated tower built in 1912 by local labour given freely. On the north side a United Free Church now in retirement serves as an agricultural building. Just by the junction is the beautiful Church of Scotland church (1790) and burial ground with its memorial to Betty Mouat and Mainland's Stores (supermarket, post office and fuel). Cycle north passing Dunrossness Community Hall and take the junction left to Skelberry. There is an excellent burnt mound site on the right by a burn shortly after the junction before one climbs past the Methodist Chapel. Near here I commented on the number and diversity of churches in the area to two men I met on the road, "Yes", I was solemnly told, "We Ness men are always on our knees praying for one thing or another!"

To visit the broch at Lunabister take the junction left marked Longfield and swing right to follow the road to where it ends near Loch of Spiggie and Broch Cottage.

Climb back up to the road and continue towards South Scousburgh turning left at Spiggie Lodge (B&B) and Spiggie Hotel to descend to the start point.

CIRCULAR WALK F

FITFUL HEAD (Old Norse: 'Vitafjall' – 'Beacon Hill')
6 miles (10 kms) : 4 hours

OS Maps: **Landranger Sheet 4 Shetland – South Mainland**
Pathfinder Sheet HU 31/41 Sumburgh

Fitful Head is one of the most dramatic headlands in Shetland. Here peregrine falcons nested and the great white-tailed sea eagles had their eyrie. There is a stiff climb to the summit but it is well worth it to see the views, a war memorial, the scene of the 'Braer' oil tanker grounding and Quendale Mill at the walk's end.

'Da wind flanns in frae Fitful Head
Wast ower frae blatterin seas ......'
Laurence Graham

A track, which services the radar site on Fitful Head starts from the road south of Quendale. Use the track for the climb leaving it before it doglegs to the summit to walk the high cliffs of Windy Stacks, which usually live up to their name. Continue round the Nev, renowned for its caves, particularly Thief's House, and clamber up the many remains of earth embankments on the slopes of the hill. The views are so magnificent there are ample excuses for stopping to catch one's breath. On the top of Fitful Head pass the radome by the Trig. Pt. (283m) and hopefully enjoy views of both Foula and Fair Isle. Further along the cliffs is a small plateau on which stands a stone

memorial erected by the community council to the crew of an RAF Halifax bomber, which crashed here in March 1942. Descend towards Garths Ness where in a geo below the tanker 'Braer' grounded and eventually broke up in January 1993. Today no sign of the tanker is visible.

Follow a track across to Bay of Quendale where the white sandy beach (not considered suitable for swimming) can gleam in the sun. From the beach, where in 1845 1,540 whales were driven ashore, walk the road which heads north back to Quendale. It is worth stopping at Quendale

Stack o' da Noup.

Sands of Scousburgh and Fitful Head.

75

Watermill, which first milled oats and bere in 1868. It has been restored to full working order by the Shetland Amenity Trust and opened in 1993. It offers a small craft shop and refreshments. A perfect place to end this memorable walk.

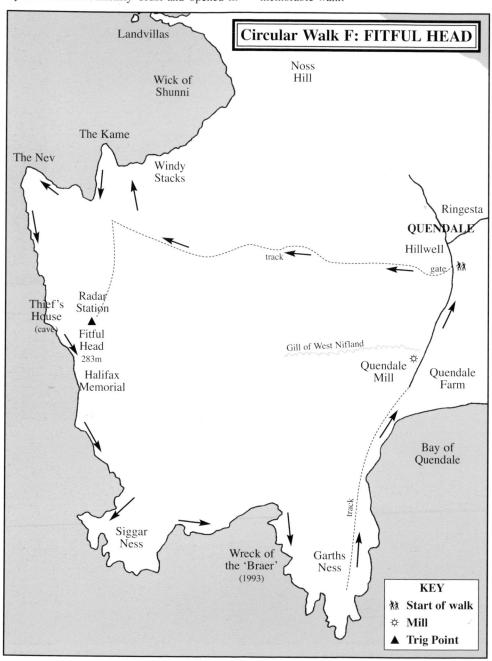

Circular Walk F: FITFUL HEAD

Landvillas

Noss Hill

Wick of Shunni

The Kame

The Nev

Windy Stacks

Ringesta

QUENDALE

Hillwell

track

gate

Thief's House (cave)

Radar Station

Fitful Head

283m

Gill of West Nifland

Halifax Memorial

Quendale Mill

Quendale Farm

Bay of Quendale

track

Siggar Ness

Wreck of the 'Braer' (1993)

Garths Ness

track

KEY

👬 **Start of walk**

☼ **Mill**

▲ **Trig Point**

Halifax memorial, Fitful Head.

Garth, Dunrossness ('cleared' in 1874).   G. W. Wilson, circa 1870

CIRCULAR WALK G ▐

SUMBURGH HEAD

2½ miles (4 kms) : 2 hours (not including Jarlshof visit)

OS Maps: **Landranger Sheet 4 Shetland – South Mainland**
Pathfinder Sheet HU 31/41 Sumburgh

Sumburgh Head from the air.

A heritage and wildlife climb up the road to imposing Sumburgh Head lighthouse from Jarlshof, Shetland's internationally famous historic site with ruins dating from Neolithic times to the 16th century. Look for whales and dolphins offshore and a whole variety of nesting seabirds on the cliffs up to the lighthouse.

In the grounds of the Sumburgh Hotel one can park and gain access to Jarlshof, an archaeological site spanning 3000 years of

The author at the tip of Sumburgh Head.

settlement. Historic Scotland have care of the site where there is an interpretive centre and an excellent guidebook is available. The shifting sands have been formally excavated to reveal a variety of prehistoric dwellings, a broch and a Norse village. There is much to explore although the site does not extend southwards as far as it did because of encroachment by the sea.

From the hotel take the road up to the headland passing a farmhouse to which is attached a kiln. Near the main car park is an information board and part of the huge skull of sperm whale on display. The cliffs have large seabird colonies, which can be seen by standing on convenient ledges. The RSPB display board tells of puffins (2000 pairs), guillemots, fulmars, shags, kittiwakes and razorbills. In the lighthouse compound make for the farthest corner, beyond the horn, and view Sumburgh Head. The lighthouse, now automatic, was built in 1821 by Thomas Stevenson.

On the site of the lighthouse there could have

been an Iron Age promontory fort. Some stony ramparts and ditches on the approach to the headland survived until 1968 when a new road was built.

Walk back down the road leaving it to climb up to the radar station near Compass Head. Keep well away from the cliff edge and make for a stone wall. Between this wall and the next the cliff has walled ramparts. Go round the radome

and descend the slope past a war time shelter to reach a pebbly beach at Grutness. A telephone box and toilets will be found at the jetty at Grutness Voe, which is the ferry terminal for Fair Isle.

Follow the road back to the Sumburgh Hotel passing a lighthouse related building with an inscription stating 'To Lighthouse 1 mile and 1033 yards'.

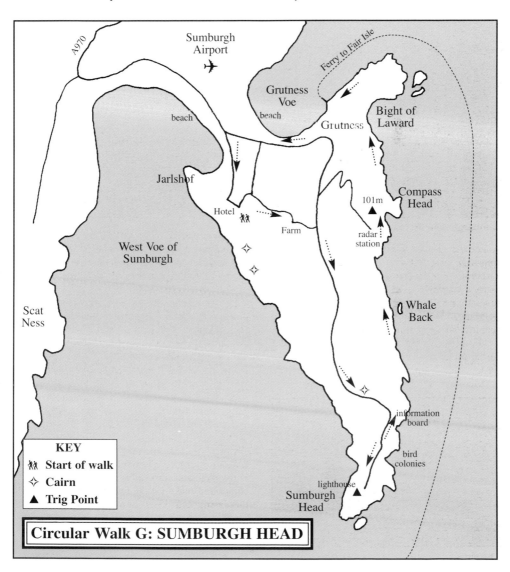

Circular Walk G: SUMBURGH HEAD

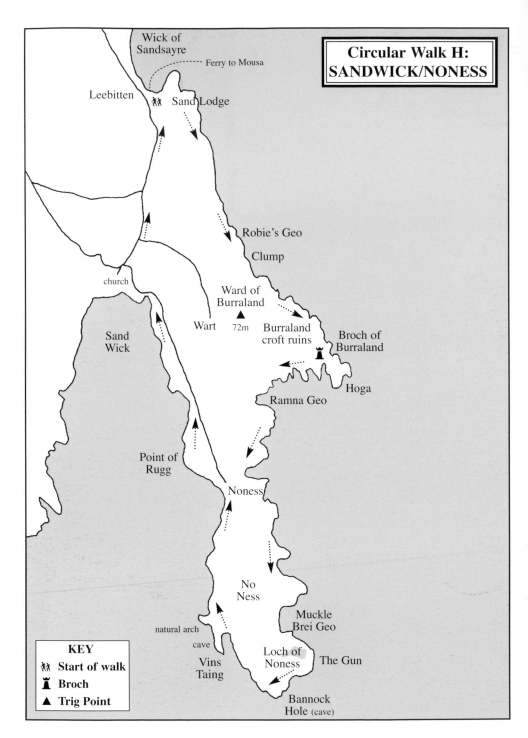

Circular Walk H:
SANDWICK/NONESS

Wick of
Sandsayre

Ferry to Mousa

Leebitten

Sand Lodge

Robie's Geo

Clump

church

Ward of
Burraland

Wart   72m   Burraland
croft ruins   Broch of
Burraland

Sand
Wick

Hoga

Ramna Geo

Point of
Rugg

Noness

No
Ness

Muckle
Brei Geo

natural arch

cave

Vins
Taing

Loch of
Noness   The Gun

Bannock
Hole (cave)

KEY
Start of walk
Broch
Trig Point

CIRCULAR WALK H

SANDWICK – NONESS
6 miles (9.5 kms) : 3 hours

OS Maps: **Landranger Sheet 4 Shetland – South Mainland**
Pathfinder Sheet HU 32/42 Sandwick

A heritage walk passing through an area of 19th century copper mining to ancient and impressive broch ruins at Burraland. A most attractive picnic spot will be found on No Ness near a popular basking area for seals.

From the Wick of Sandayre where sailing dinghies are drawn up by the slipway in summer, walk east round the walled garden of impressive Sand Lodge. The grass verges on the edge of the banks takes one past a small turreted tower to an interesting group of outbuildings. It is quickly clear that one is going to enjoy a view of the west coast of Mousa on this walk. Pass a small curved roofed brick built building with a chimney hole and walk round Robie's Geo and Clump. Above is Trig. Pt. on the Ward of Burraland (72m), which affords superb all round views of the area.

The notable Broch of Burraland will be found beyond an area of extensive croft ruins and is approached past a stone sheepfold at the base of the mound on which it sits. The site lies on a plateau between two geos and an iron-age settlement site is immediately to its south. We are virtually opposite the broch on Mousa and the location makes this spot one of the most appealing picnic spots in Shetland. The several geos of Noness are the background to the walk round Hoga. The next beach has various stone ruins on it including a standing stone surrounded by rubble. Seals bask on the flat rocks and porpoises may be seen fishing.

There are four helpful stiles to get one onto the top of the ness where there is rich meadowland. Exercise great caution – the cliffs are precipitous and crumbly. Round Muckle Brei Geo is a freshwater loch, a popular basking place for birds and The Gun presumably something once associated with an octagonal concrete base at the point of the Ness.

Descend to the next geo where a slanted cave named Bannock Hole can be seen on the

Burraland Croft, Noness. South Mousa beyond.

Broch, Burraland, with Mousa Broch opposite.

western bank. We are now almost opposite the Levenwick Broch. The mound of stones is just discernible. Climb round to a well-built wall but just before reaching it look down west to view two natural arches on a stack close inshore. It resembles an elephant on a sloping stand. The cliffs now are in marked contrast to those walking south being low level and give an excellent view of Sandwick Church and the township beyond.

Burraland Croft, Noness. North Mousa beyond.

Pass a square ruined enclosure, mining spoil heaps and a concrete lined well. Immediately after a second spoil heap pass through ornamental gateposts down to the first house on the road. A stile will be found after a huge lump of tussock grass adjacent to a gate. Admire the green surrounds to a restored well at Noness croft before heading round a small geo with a boat winch on it near Point of Rugg. Take the road past the church and then head straight north back to Sand Lodge.

Copper mining started in Shetland in 1789 when Alexander Creighton of Tynemouth discovered copper prospects at Sand Lodge. In 1790 a party of Welsh miners came to Shetland and mined 12 tons of ore which left Shetland in September. In 1800 a party of Cornish miners were employed and Richard Trevithick, the famous Cornish engineer, was engaged to supply a steam engine. The mine was not a success and much of the ore obtained came from near surface deposits. Throughout the 1800s money was wasted putting down shafts to a rich lode that probably does not exist. In the 1920s a company was floated to work the mine but no mining seems to have actually taken place.

CIRCULAR WALK I

MOUSA
4 miles (6.5 kms) : 3 hours

OS Maps: **Landranger Sheet 4 Shetland – South Mainland**
Pathfinder Sheet HU 32/42 Sandwick

Mousa is a must. The uninhabited island has the most romantic and complete ruined broch in Britain and is remarkable both by day and on summer nights when trips are specially made to hear and see the storm petrels. These sea birds nest both in the broch and the boulder beach nearby. A tidal pool on the East Side lures seals at low tide which gives marvelous opportunities for watching them.

In summer a boat service to Mousa is operated by Tom Jamieson (Tel: 01595 431367) from the pier at Leebitton. Trips are weather dependent and no dogs are allowed. Mousa is not without its wrecks. On 10th April 1930 the Lerwick – Aberdeen ferry the St. Sunniva was wrecked on Mousa, fortunately with no loss of life, when in fog it hit submerged rocks between Muckle Bard and The Swarf.

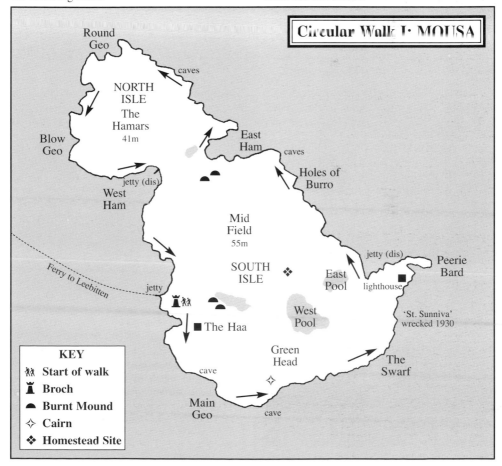

Circular Walk I · MOUSA

Round Geo

caves

NORTH ISLE
The Hamars
41m

Blow Geo

East Ham

caves

Holes of Burro

jetty (dis)

West Ham

Mid Field
55m

jetty (dis)

Peerie Bard

Ferry to Leebitten

jetty

SOUTH ISLE

East Pool

lighthouse

'St. Sunniva' wrecked 1930

West Pool

The Haa

Green Head

The Swarf

cave

Main Geo

cave

KEY
- 👫 **Start of walk**
- 🗼 **Broch**
- ⏴ **Burnt Mound**
- ✧ **Cairn**
- ❖ **Homestead Site**

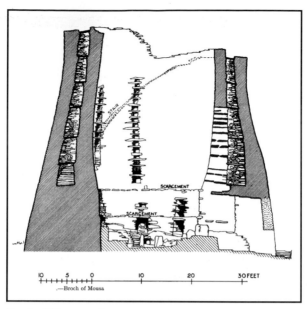

Broch of Mousa – plan.

We land just below the broch which stands 43ft (13m) high and is built in local schistose slate. It has chambers, galleries, an internal staircase and an open parapet, all now visible after the interior was completely cleared of debris in 1919. It stands on a low promontory originally surrounded by a wall at some 20ft distance, now reduced to foundation level. At its lowest level the broch has an internal diameter of some 20ft and the wall varies in thickness from 15 to 17ft. There is no record of its defensive features ever being put to the test apart from the year 1153. The Viking 'Egil's Saga' states that about the year AD900 an eloping couple from Norway, Bjørn and Thora, were shipwrecked on Shetland on their way to Iceland, took refuge and married in the broch. A similar incident is recorded in the 'Orkneyinga Saga' when in 1153 a certain young Erlend carried off Margaret, Earl Harold Maddadson's mother, from Orkney to Shetland and settled down with the lady and his band of followers in Mousa, where he laid in stores. Earl Harold followed and laid siege to the broch but found it, "an unhandy place to get at", by storm. The episode ended in reconciliation and Erlend married Margaret. Signs of earlier inhabitation on the island will be found 250 yards ENE of the broch where there are two burnt mounds by the loch and another at Mid Field on the N. slopes 150 yards from the shore at East Ham, crescentic 1m (h).

Although the island has not been inhabited for about a hundred years there are many ruinous buildings such as The Haa and stone enclosures to be seen. These mostly date from the 17th and 18th Century.

Continue round Masti Geo and climb Green Head to West Pool and East Pool, which are excellent places to watch common seals.

The old lighthouse by Peerie Bard was once serviced by the small jetty and a new lighthouse has now been established. Aim up the coastline taking care to avoid falling into the Holes of Burro by walking inland. The North Isle is also an excellent place to watch, at a distance, the activities of a tern colony. The gentle stroll takes us round to the redundant jetty at West Ham and back onto South Isle. One can easily enjoy a day on Mousa and if the stay can be extended into the late evening to see the petrels circle the ancient walls of Mousa broch then every opportunity should be taken to do so.

CIRCULAR WALK J ▮

NESS OF SOUND
3 miles (5 kms) : 2 hours

OS Maps: **Landranger Sheet 4 Shetland – South Mainland**
Pathfinder Sheet HU 44/54 Lerwick

A good walk on which to enjoy sights of wading birds and ducks. Views of Bressay and Lerwick and at the end of the Ness an eerie area of World War 2 gun emplacements.

At the roundabout near the Safeway supermarket take the road signed 'Ness of Sound'.

There is a large car park by the sports ground at Seafield. From there walk up Kantersted Road turning left up a narrow lane. Follow the road right; it becomes a hard core track, which we leave by a stile on the left, before it reaches the house at the end of the track. Walk across the sand and shingle beach to climb through a fence below the large Seafield House.

Head east along the Ness, a sturdy stile brings one by excellent grazing land enjoyed by sheep and cattle belonging to the farm standing on the slope of the hill. The rocky foreshore is popular with small shellfish particularly cockles as mounds of empty shells testify. Pass a concrete/stone-ruined building but when the sight of Bard Head on Bressay comes into view ahead start climbing up to a grey rocky escarpment. The cliffs of the point of the Ness are quite deceptive and on the escarpment are various cracks and fissure to be avoided. On top are various sections of concrete hardstanding once used to site signal masts on. From here view rafts of tysties and sometimes fishermen hauling in lobster creels.

Walk down to a fence on the cliff edge facing Bressay and follow it to an area of World War 2 gun emplacements and bunkers; one is

Ness of Sound gun emplacements.

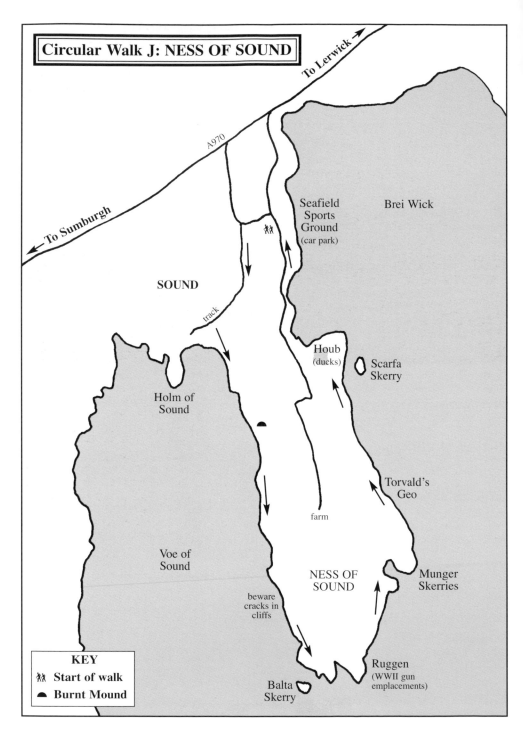

Circular Walk J: NESS OF SOUND

To Lerwick →

To Sumburgh ←

A970

SOUND

Seafield Sports Ground (car park)

Brei Wick

track

Holm of Sound

Houb (ducks)

Scarfa Skerry

Torvald's Geo

farm

Voe of Sound

NESS OF SOUND

Munger Skerries

beware cracks in cliffs

Ruggen (WWII gun emplacements)

Balta Skerry

KEY

🚶🚶 **Start of walk**

◣ **Burnt Mound**

Town Hall and war memorial, Lerwick.

particularly perilously perched on the cliff edge now. All rather ghostly.

There are superb views of Lerwick which stretch from the red roof of the Clickimin Sports complex to the solid stone of Lerwick Town Hall tower and the Knab. Continue past various dug outs and walk slightly inland to avoid three small geos in quick succession. Follow a stone wall down to a fenced off stone embankment and area containing a decayed storage tanks. At the end of the fence there is just room to squeeze between it and a stone wall to get access to a tarmac road at a turning point. In a small houb you may sight ducks (mainly mallard) and geese enjoying this feature. On our left note an avenue of trees running along the access road to Seafield House and at Seafield Lodge a rowing boat is seeing out retirement on the lawn as a raised flower bed. Turn left to go past the Edward Thomason Home and return to the car park.

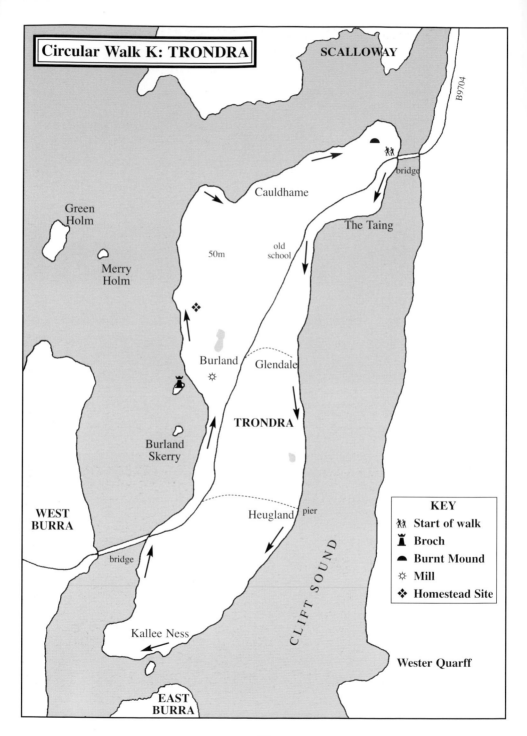

Circular Walk K: TRONDRA

SCALLOWAY

B9704

Cauldhame

bridge

The Taing

Green
Holm

50m

old
school

Merry
Holm

Burland

Glendale

Burland
Skerry

TRONDRA

WEST
BURRA

Heugland

pier

bridge

CLIFT SOUND

Kallee Ness

Wester Quarff

EAST
BURRA

KEY

👫 **Start of walk**

⚱ **Broch**

⬛ **Burnt Mound**

☼ **Mill**

❖ **Homestead Site**

CIRCULAR WALK K ▀▀▀▀▀▀▀▀▀▀▀▀▀▀▀▀

TRONDRA

6½ miles (11 kms) : 3 hours (not including Burland visit)

OS Maps: **Landranger Sheet 4 Shetland – South Mainland**
                          Pathfinder Sheet HU 33 Scalloway

A delightful low level walk round one of Shetland's smaller inhabited islands from the bridge to Mainland.

The bridge connecting Mainland Shetland to Trondra opened in 1971 and it had an immediate and profound impact not only on Trondra but also on Burra folk for whom it became a stepping stone. From the bridge walk south above the Taing and survey an attractive garden and neat small boat jetty on the shore at Hiogaland.

Leave the road as it moves inland before reaching the former school on the right, its high playground walls still intact, to pass the crofts at Glendale and Heughland where the pier faces cross Clift Sound to the hills rising towards Wester Quarff. Kallee Ness is an area of old settlements and from it head north past salmon cages to cross the road at the Burra bridge and make for Burland. Time should be allowed for a visit to Burland where the Shetland Croft Trail allows the opportunity to see Shetland breeds of livestock, crofting history, a restored watermill and Shetland boat building. One Shetland boat is a foureen nearly 120 years old and I can vouch for its sea worthiness having gone to the Eela Fishing Competition in Burravoe, Yell, with Tammy Isbister in the 1980s.

At Burland use the footbridge to cross over the burn which powers the restored water mill. The foureen, built in 1880, may be seen hauled up into a noost. Just offshore, on an islet, are the ruins of a broch. The islet is linked to Trondra by a stone causeway.

A little further north is the loch and Pund of Burland, which is a Neolithic homestead site. Head up the slopes to the highest point on Trondra (50m) leaving the green grazing land when climbing over a fence onto rough pasture. After passing a small cairn walk down to the modern Cauldhame housing development. From here follow the shore round the northern promontory, which contains a burnt mound oval, 5m x 2.5m x 0.4m, to pass an old jetty and the electricity cable landfall and climb up to the bridge.

Tammy and Mary Isbister with 100 year old foureen.

The islands of West Burra and East Burra contain a fascinating variety of attractions both in scenery, in historical sites and in modern living. Rather than describe a linear route round them (West Burra 14 miles (22km) approx. East Burra 12 miles (19km) approx.) I have suggested two circular walks on East Burra and three on West Burra.

The islands have much to offer the walker who will have many opportunities also to observe bird and mammal life both inland and on the shore. The wildlife could include the menfolk who, if the warring spirit moves them, will perform the 'Burra Isle Mens' War Dance'. A vigorous jig, it is popularly performed to the tune 'The Marchioness of Tillybardy'. The origins of the dance are obscure but it may be related to a dance observed in Newfoundland during the period of the Greenland whaling.

It may also be of comfort to know that here are the most devout otters in Shetland. A family of otters was discovered to be happily living in the roof of the Methodist Chapel in West Burra. Despite this laudable display of nonconformity the otters were eventually encouraged to pursue their devotions elsewhere.

Otters join the congregation at the Methodist Chapel in West Burra.   **Jennifer Nisbet**

CIRCULAR WALK L

WEST BURRA – SANDS OF MEAL TO HAMNAVOE
3½ miles (6 kms) : 2 hours

OS Maps: **Landranger Sheet 4 Shetland – South Mainland**
Pathfinder Sheet HU 33 Scalloway

Hamnavoe is the largest settlement in Burra and there is evidence that it has always been a place of habitation. This lovely coastal walk covers historic sites, a lighthouse and the centre of this important Shetland fishing community.

From the car park (toilets) above the Sands of Meal walk down the public access path to one of Shetland's finest beaches and a favourite picnic spot. Note the cliff side burial place of a sailor, "Known unto God" marked by a blue

cross erected in 1917. Follow the banks north east to walk below Branchiclett where a prehistoric underground structure, a subterranean passage, was unearthed and there are three burnt mounds, 1 crescentic and 2 circular. At Lu Ness is a settlement site and by a burn two burnt mounds. Climb up to Biargar and look for a large rock moved by violent wave action on which is painted the date 19/12/91. Head north and look down on the original, natural, swimming pool in a cleft of

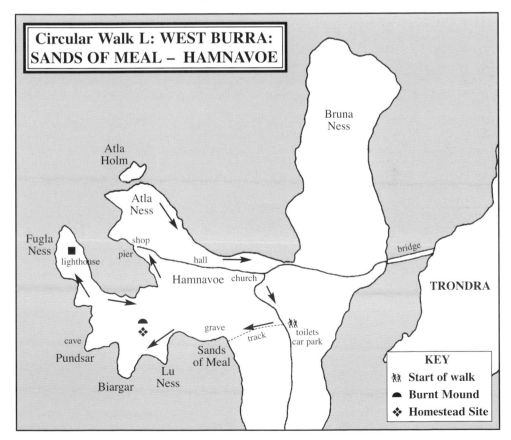

Circular Walk L: WEST BURRA:
SANDS OF MEAL – HAMNAVOE

Bruna Ness

Atla Holm

Atla Ness

Fugla Ness

shop

pier

lighthouse

hall

bridge

Hamnavoe church

TRONDRA

grave

toilets
car park

track

cave

Sands of Meal

Pundsar

Lu Ness

Biargar

KEY

Start of walk

Burnt Mound

Homestead Site

Seaman's grave, Sands of Meal, West Burra.

the rocks below, concreted at its northern end. Countless children first swam here in what was affectionately known as the 'Muckle Loch'. A large cave visible below the next headland, Pundsar, is accessible by those daring enough by clambering through a crack in the cliff on the other side of the promontory. There is a helpful rope but it all looked too forbidding to me! A prominent stone enclosure stands on top of the cliff (an otter trap?) from which descend to commence boulder bashing out to the sonar panelled powered lighthouse on Fugla Ness. Return passing the now redundant steps once used for servicing it and head round the bay passing Coopers Pier and a 'Viking roundhouse' erected as a school project in 1960 to reach Halcrow's General Stores, toilets and main pier of Hamnavoe.

Burra Isle keeps the tradition of fishing alive

and the beaches of Hamnavoe were used for curing cod in the early 19th century. In 1845 a large fish-curing shed was built and later a kippering kiln – emphasising Hamnavoe's importance as a herring port in the early part of the season. Today a modern fleet continues the tradition.

Walk round Atla Ness and look north to Papa Isle and see if you can spot the remains of the kirk above Muckle Ayre. Climb up towards the houses and the modern community hall to join the road. At the junction below the church a yoag shell dump (large mussels used as bait) is visible in the turf by which we turn south to return to the start point.

This walk can be extended to include Bruna Ness, the 2 mile (3km) route described in Circular Walk O.

CIRCULAR WALK M
WEST BURRA – BRIDGE END TO RUFF LOCH AND PAPIL
4 miles (6 kms) : 2 hours

OS Maps: **Landranger Sheet 4 Shetland – South Mainland**
Pathfinder Sheet HU 33 Scalloway

The cliffs of Hill of Sandwick are in marked contrast to the ancient settlement area round Ruff Loch. The walk is completed by visiting the ancient ecclesiastical site at Papil and the stubborn standing stone on Mid Field.

From the Church of Scotland church at Bridge End take the road past modern houses to a track ("Horses at Foot" warning) leading to the croft at Sandwick. Walk the south side of the Bay of Sand Wick before climbing up Hill of Sandwick, which becomes increasingly rocky. The hill contains a natural arch, which can be viewed, just, as one rounds Ramna Geo. The natural arch on Stack of Sandwick has to be viewed when some distance away. The rocky

area is popular with sea birds and oyster-catchers. Whale Wick is most impressive from which cross fence where a gap in the wire has been made to walk down to Ruff Loch. At the north end water leaves the loch to make a waterfall down the cliffs and there is slight evidence of a watermill. More obvious, on the cliff edge, is the eleven stoned cairn (the Ill Craig) perhaps all that is left of a promontory fort? There is a large collection of other stone collections round the loch from which walk up the cliff edge, keeping well in, to the large cairn, a former fishing meid, at Virda (56m). To the east are planticrubs on the slope of the hill and the roofless Haa at Houss surveys West Voe. Walk down through pasture to the left of Loch

Theo Fullerton by possible promontory fort, Ruff Loch.

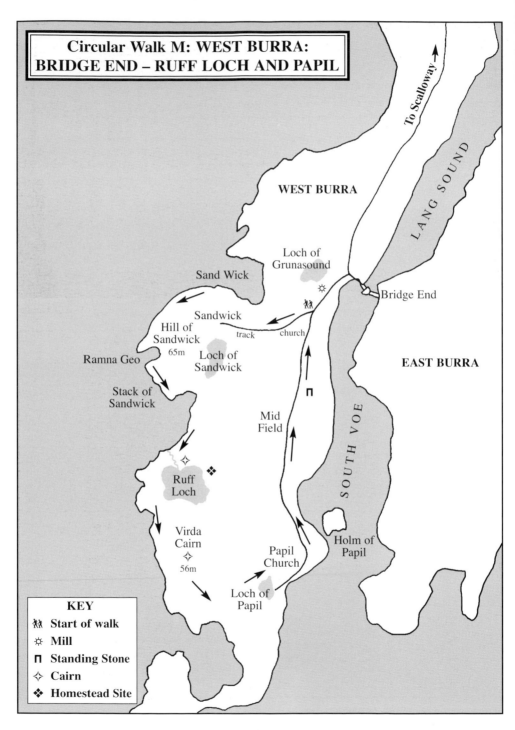

Circular Walk M: WEST BURRA: BRIDGE END – RUFF LOCH AND PAPIL

WEST BURRA

To Scalloway→

LANG SOUND

Loch of Grunasound

Sand Wick

Bridge End

Sandwick

church

track

EAST BURRA

Hill of Sandwick

65m

Loch of Sandwick

Ramna Geo

Stack of Sandwick

Mid Field

SOUTH VOE

Ruff Loch

Virda Cairn

56m

Holm of Papil

Papil Church

Loch of Papil

KEY

ⵜ **Start of walk**

☼ **Mill**

П **Standing Stone**

✧ **Cairn**

❖ **Homestead Site**

Monk's Stone. Dennis Coutts

of Papil to visit the roofless Papil kirk, dedicated to St. Lawrence. On this site three early Christian carved stones were found in the graveyard two of which, the Monk's stone and an early Christian cross slab, and a replica of the Papil stone gravemarker are displayed in the Shetland Museum, Lerwick.

The Monk's stone depicts four cowled figures and one cowled horseman approaching a stone cross on a decorated relief which I interpret as the sea. They could be Irish missionaries who were known to wear a long coarse outer woolen garment over a white tunic. They were tonsured (shaved) on the front of the head and wore their hair long at the back. They often coloured parts of their bodies, especially the eyelids, which were painted black. They used long walking sticks, leather water bottles and wallets for their books and relics.

In 816 the Council of Chelsea legislated against wandering Irish clerics so perhaps some settled down at Papil and other places bearing the name in Shetland – Papil Isle, Papa Stour, Papil Ness (Yell) and Papil Water (Fetlar). However, Raymond Lamb considers that, "the sculptured stones from Papil suggest contacts with the east, not the west side of Britain; their art is

Papil Stone.

Pictish, and is suggestive of that eighth-century period when the Pictish church itself was under Northumbrian influence".

Follow the road north and visit the standing stone to the east of the road on Mid Field from which is a splendid view of the Bridge End outdoor centre and marina. The stone is of irregular shape of native rock with quartz veins. It rises to a height of 6ft 8ins and is 5ft 2ins broad. The slight hollow in which the stone stands could indicate some attempt to move it. Tradition tells that there was an attempt to break it up for building purposes when the nearby church was built. However, the monument resisted all efforts to change its location!

At Bridge End note the remains of watermills on the slope to the east side of the road once powered by water from the Loch of Grunasound.

Standing stone, West Burra, Bridge End beyond.

CIRCULAR WALK N ▰▰▰▰▰▰▰▰▰
WEST BURRA – PAPIL TO BANNA MINN AND KETTLA NESS
5 miles (8 kms) : 3 hours

OS Maps: **Landranger Sheet 4 Shetland – South Mainland**
Pathfinder Sheet HU 33 Scalloway
HU 32 Sandwick

A walk to a brilliant Atlantic sandy storm beach and a rugged headland with fine views, seals and, in season, colonies of arctic skuas and arctic terns.

From Papil, an ancient Christian site and present burial ground, walk the road south past one of the few remaining thatched croft houses, at Duncanslate. Take a footpath down to the beach, which can be crossed on a turf track. The views of the sea crashing into the Bay of Banna Minn past the Black Stacks, particularly in a south west gale, can be most impressive. Pass the cottage at Minn and climb up onto the western banks – dramatic cliffs, which contain various caves, natural arches and stacks. Sadly,

on Fugla Stack, the German fishing boat 'Castor' was lost with all hands 17th February 1910. The 'Castor' was known in Burra as the "sweetie wreck" due to the number of tins of peppermints that were washed up from the wreck. The lochs at Virda Vatn and Annyeruss will be seen enroute to the Trig. Pt. at the peak of Kettla Ness (48m). Marvellous views here of South Havra and the main coastline. Descend to pass Croo Loch and Outra Loch which once powered the now derelict water mills in the burn flowing down from the loch to Groot Ness. Head back round the Bight of Sandy Geos and return from the ness by the ayre crossed earlier. Keep clear of any tern colonies encountered on the way.

Thatched croft, Duncanslate, Burra.

Circular Walk N: WEST BURRA:
PAPIL – BANNA MINN AND KETTLE NESS

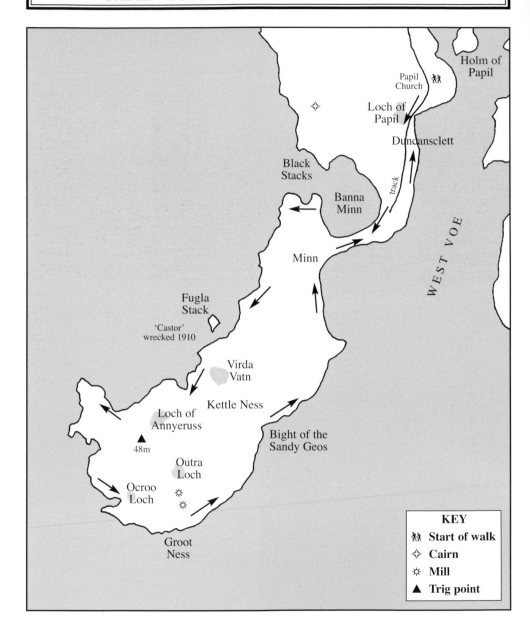

Holm of Papil

Papil Church

Loch of Papil

Duncansclett

Black Stacks

Banna Minn

Minn

WEST VOE

track

Fugla Stack

'Castor' wrecked 1910

Virda Vatn

Kettle Ness

Loch of Annyeruss

48m

Bight of the Sandy Geos

Outra Loch

Ocroo Loch

Groot Ness

KEY

👫 **Start of walk**

✧ **Cairn**

☼ **Mill**

▲ **Trig point**

Banna Minn beach, Burra.

CIRCULAR WALK O

WEST BURRA – SETTER TO BRUNNA NESS

2 miles (3 kms) : 1 hour

OS Maps: **Landranger Sheet 4 Shetland – South Mainland**
Pathfinder Sheet HU 33 Scalloway

A short walk climbing up to the distinctive cairn and Giant's Stone on Bruna Ness with its secret beach and taking in a prehistoric settlement site and more cairns on the return.

A road leads off the B9074 to a small group of houses at Setter. From here descend green slopes of pasture to a small bay and climb up to follow a fence to the north cairn (59m). Great views of the coastline and partial views of Scalloway. Descend north east to a massive boulder 'The Giant's Stone' which measures approximately 15ft by 9ft. Below it is an accessible if remote beach, which must be a

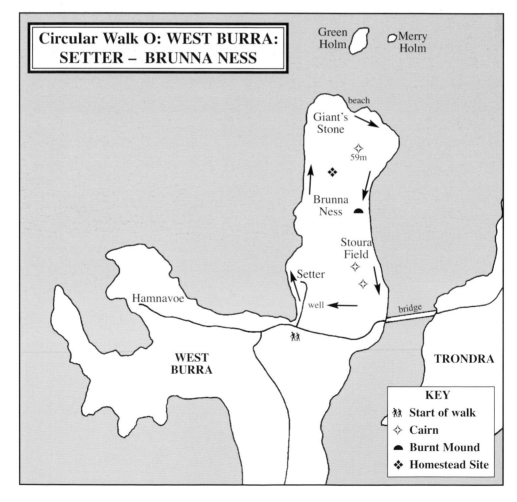

Circular Walk O: WEST BURRA: SETTER – BRUNNA NESS

Green Holm

Merry Holm

beach

Giant's Stone

59m

Brunna Ness

Stoura Field

Setter

well

bridge

Hamnavoe

WEST BURRA

TRONDRA

KEY
👥 **Start of walk**
✧ **Cairn**
⏵ **Burnt Mound**
❖ **Homestead Site**

most attractive place to be on a summer's day. Walk to take the east coast back noting an interesting 'cheesering' rocky outcrop before walking down to the small plain of Stoura Field. Planticrubs dominate the shore line and salmon cages just offshore. Opposite them is a Neolithic homestead site identified by a circular ring of stones. Five burnt mound sites of various sizes will be found in the marshy ground below a spring. Make a beeline for the next cairn, to avoid the precipitous cliff, from which make slight descent to a third cairn. From here return to Setter noting a well with hinged cover near the road.

Giant's Stone, Brunna Ness, West Burra.

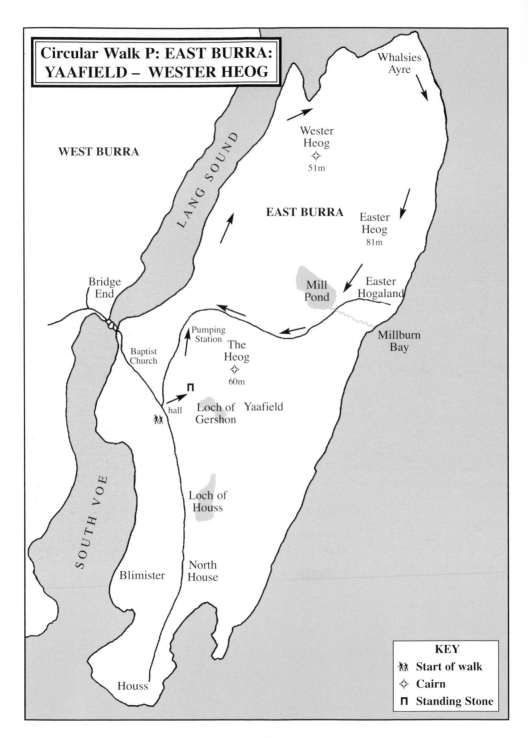

Circular Walk P: EAST BURRA: YAAFIELD – WESTER HEOG

WEST BURRA

LANG SOUND

Whalsies Ayre

Wester Heog
✧
51m

EAST BURRA

Easter Heog
81m

Bridge End

Mill Pond

Easter Hogaland

Millburn Bay

Pumping Station

Baptist Church

The Heog
✧
60m

Π

hall

Loch of Gershon

Yaafield

SOUTH VOE

Loch of Houss

Blimister

North House

Houss

KEY
🚶 **Start of walk**
✧ **Cairn**
Π **Standing Stone**

CIRCULAR WALK P

EAST BURRA – YAA FIELD TO WESTER HEOG
3½ miles (6 kms) : 2 hours

OS Maps: **Landranger Sheet 4 Shetland – South Mainland**
Pathfinder Sheet HU 33 Scalloway

One of the finest panoramas of the islands will be seen on this walk which includes an ancient standing stone and two massive Neolithic stone cairns.

Start the walk at the Bridge End Public Hall by walking the road, signposted East Hogaland, for about 100 yards. Head east to follow a wire fence to where the standing stone of Yaa Field stands in front of a square planticrub. It is 7ft tall in what is an area of ancient settlement – seven burnt mounds have been identified in the Houlls, Loch of Gershon, Norbister area. The stone is an irregularly shaped quartz-veined boulder and at the base, which has been packed, it is 3ft 3ins broad.

Standing stone, East Burra. Royl Field beyond.

Return to the road leaving it at the junction to the water pumping station to head north to the cairn of massive stones now scattered at a height of 51m. The ground gradually slopes away north to Whalsies Ayre from which ascend to Easter Heog hill (81m). Walk down to Mill Pond, which once powered water mills and for years was the reservoir for Burra, and join the road. Head west leaving the road to climb The Heog where a very dilapidated cairn (60m) covers an area of 70ft in diameter and therefore it must have been originally of considerable size. A final view can be appreciated from the pumping station before descending back down the road to the start point.

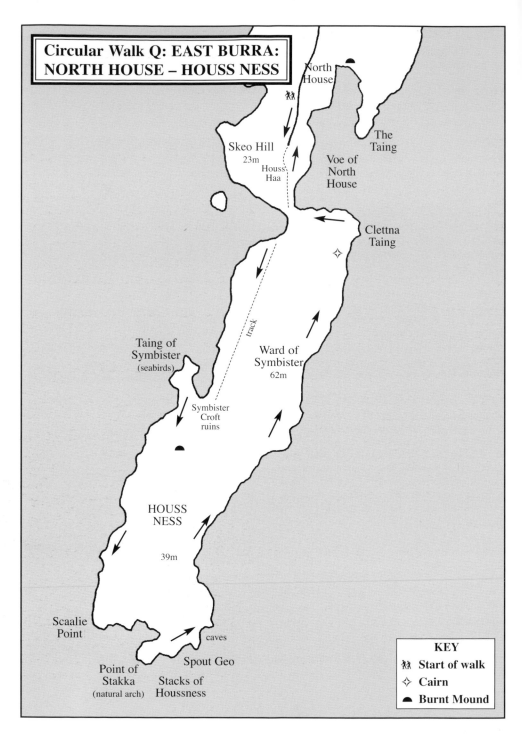

Circular Walk Q: EAST BURRA: NORTH HOUSE – HOUSS NESS

North House

The Taing

Skeo Hill
23m

Houss
Haa

Voe of
North
House

Clettna
Taing

track

Taing of
Symbister
(seabirds)

Ward of
Symbister
62m

Symbister
Croft
ruins

HOUSS
NESS
39m

Scaalie
Point

caves

Point of
Stakka
(natural arch)

Spout Geo

Stacks of
Houssness

KEY

🚶 **Start of walk**

✧ **Cairn**

⬤ **Burnt Mound**

CIRCULAR WALK Q

EAST BURRA – NORTH HOUSE TO HOUSS NESS

5 miles (8 kms) : 3 hours

OS Maps: **Landranger Sheet 4 Shetland – South Mainland**
                    Pathfinder Sheet HU 33 Scalloway
                    HU 32 Sandwick

Follow the road past the croft at Northouse which stands on a splendid site above the Voe of North House, today a place of salmon farm activity but once an area of ancient habitation, as indicated by a crescentic burnt mound at the head of the voe. Head south along the road to the road end and park on land near the ruined, roofless Haa of Houss. On Skeo Hill (23m) adjacent, south, to the Haa was once an early structure on this prominent hillock. A kitchen midden close by yielded pottery and stone objects similar to those found in broch sites. The Haa, once the mansion of the Sinclair family, was last occupied in about 1910 when it housed several families. The large stone roof tiles were removed from within the house. Go through a gate and follow a grassy track down to Ayre Dyke, which is covered with flotsam brought in on the tide. Go through a gate and continue along the track towards the deserted croft site at Symbister. The tenants had once hoped to build a proper road access to Symbister but funds ran out in the early 1930s so it was never completed.

Symbister is the sort of site I have fantasised about. It is a superb location and today attracts a variety of sea bird and water activity in the waters around it. The croft was eventually abandoned in the early 1950s largely because there was no road to it.

To the south of the croft are three burnt mound sites and I am sure the area would reveal more evidence of early occupation if a formal archeological survey was ever carried out.

Walk south along the heathery west banks to go round Scaalie Point. There are caves in the headland and a fine natural arch in the distinctive Point of Stakka. From Spout Geo climb round the east banks eventually to reach the highest point of Houss Ness at the Ward of Symbister (62m). Descend north-east to Clettna Taing where on a wedge of land close to the edge of the rocky beach is a large square planticrub adjacent to a much dilapidated cairn site. Walk past more stone enclosures to reach Ayre Dyke to cross it and return along up the track to the Haa of Houss.

Joanne and Sam Christie, Northhouse, with lamb.

FAIR ISLE – INTRODUCTION

(Old Norse 'Fridarey' – 'peaceful isle')
Ferry from Grutness (J. Stout 01595 760222)
By air: Loganair (01595 840246)

Fair Isle has a warm, welcoming and friendly atmosphere where approximately 70 people renowned for their hospitality live. The island has some magnificent scenery, historical sites, resident and migratory birds and 150,000 sea birds in the summer. Although the island is only 3 miles (6 km) by 1½ miles (3 km) it provides a great opportunity for some wonderful walking. For this reason I recommend a visit to Fair Isle to last for at least three days, as it is impossible to do it justice on a day return.

Whether you fly (1/2 an hour) or take the ferry (2 hours plus) the journey to Fair Isle is a memorable experience. However, only by sea, turbulent crossing though it can be, can all that the journey has to offer be fully appreciated and there are often sightings of dolphins and other cetaceans such as porpoises, humpback whale, minkie whale and orca.

Reminders that Fair Isle has always attracted habitation will be seen in the existence of an Iron Age promontory fort, watermill systems for example at Funniquoy on the Burn of Gilsetter (old mill, shirva and new mill) and notable burnt mounds. The mound at Vaasetter is a massive 88ft by 122ft in area and as much as 10ft high! Small burial mounds near Funniquoy Mill were excavated to reveal urns now in the National Museum.

The two suggested circular walks are both the same length (5 miles/8km) and between them cover the whole coastline. Keep some time to visit the museum, shop, churches and craft shop in the south end and the Bird Observatory in the north (tel: 01595 760258).

CIRCULAR WALK R

FAIR ISLE LODGE – SOUTH HARBOUR
5 miles (8 kms) : 3 hours

OS Maps: **Landranger Sheet 4 Shetland – South Mainland**
Pathfinder Sheet HY 75/85 Fair Isle

A walk which covers the southern coastline of Fair Isle and from which it is possible to enjoy the area of the island where the community lives. The George Waterson Centre and Museum could be the first place to visit in Fair Isle but if time cannot be allowed to do so during this walk then plan on visiting it and the other attractions in this area later during your stay.

From the Lodge first visit the Landberg Iron Age promontory fort, the remains of which are conveniently situated on the 70ft high cliff edge in front of the Lodge at North Haven. Note that on the landward side the fort was protected by steep earthen ramparts mainly formed of small stones with intervening ditches. Within the small enclosure are signs of structures long since gone. The view down to beaches of North and South Haven may tempt you down for a dip!

Follow the coast south and observe the various nets used by the bird observatory for bird ringing and make for the holm known as Sheep Craig – a distinctive stack which rises to 443 ft.

The summer puffins first appear in Fair Isle on the south east banks at Furse and there is a burnt mound inland from South Whaleback. In

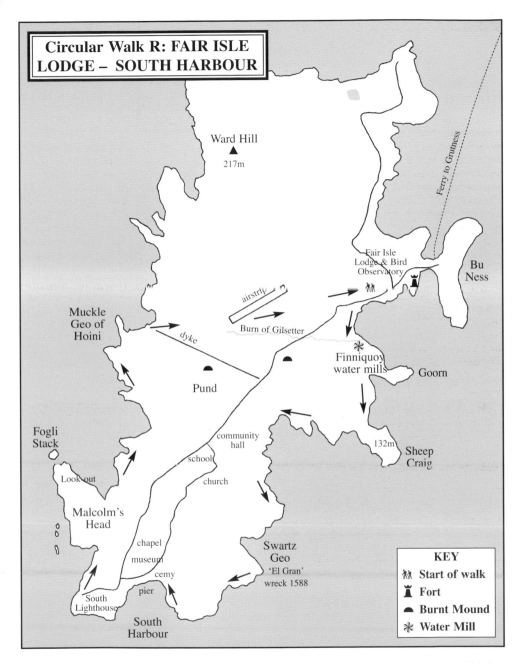

Circular Walk R: FAIR ISLE LODGE – SOUTH HARBOUR

Ward Hill
▲
217m

Ferry to Grutness

Fair Isle Lodge & Bird Observatory

Bu Ness

airstrip

Muckle Geo of Hoini

dyke

Burn of Gilsetter

Finniquoy water mills

Goorn

Pund

Fogli Stack

community hall

school

church

132m

Sheep Craig

Look-out

Malcolm's Head

chapel

museum

cemy

pier

Swartz Geo
'El Gran'
wreck 1588

South Lighthouse

South Harbour

KEY

🚶🚶 **Start of walk**

♟ **Fort**

◖ **Burnt Mound**

✳ **Water Mill**

the graveyard an iron cross commemorates the loss of the flagship on Stroms Hellier of the Spanish Armarda, the El Gran, in 1588. Tradition tells that a small chapel may once have stood in the burial ground – an adjoining creek is called Kirki Geo. The dedication of the chapel was probably to St. Peter and it produced a small revenue known as "St. Peter's

Fair Isle – Spanish Armada memorial at South Harbour. South Light beyond.

Stouk'. An old fish store has been converted into an accommodation hostel and appropriately named Puff Inn. At The Houll the aerogenerator was erected in 1982 to provide electricity to Fair Isle households. An earlier erection was a wooden flagpole standing nearly 30ft high formally used for signalling to vessels.

Boat noosts are cut into the banks near some flat stones, which, with the use of skeos, were once used for drying fish. Note the 19th century Haa where Sir Walter Scott was a guest on his visit to the Northern Isles. From the South Harbour pier visit the South Lighthouse built in 1892 and automated in 1998 before embarking on the steep climb up the CG lookout site (107m) on Malcolm's Head. This

is a dramatic headland from which to view some of the natural arches and stacks off the west coast. In the caves below men hid from the Royal Navy pressgangs in the times of the Napoleonic wars. Note the remains of the Napoleonic tower on Malcolm's Head, a now derelict stone building, three walls surviving.

At Muckle Geo of Hoini head east towards the airstrip unless wishing to take in what is thought to be Scotland's largest burnt mound north east of Pund. The mound is composed of several separate smaller mounds and measures 39m by 27m and stands 3m in height.

From the airstrip make your way back cross-country to the Lodge.

CIRCULAR WALK S

FAIR ISLE LODGE – DRONGER
5 miles (8 kms) : 3 hours

OS Maps: **Landranger Sheet 4 Shetland – South Mainland**
               Pathfinder Sheet HY 75/85 Fair Isle

Explore the coastline round the North Light, a gannet colony at Dronger and a climb up Ward hill; these are just some of many delightful prospects on this walk round the northern coastline.

Once can commence this walk by walking down past the ferry pier in North Haven to climb up South Gavel on Bu Ness (48m). Excellent views of the east coast and a Neolithic burial cairn at North Gavel. Return to the road and walk north along it until it starts to bend right. Walk west to view three burnt mounds in an ancient settlement area by the Burn of Furse. Follow the road north again leaving it to view caves, stacks and natural arches which are a feature of the north east corner of Fair Isle. The Kirn of Scroo is a subterranean passage 262 ft. long ending in a blowhole at South Raiva. The road ends at the North Light, which was built in 1891 and is now fully automated. It had a sundial to check lighting times.

In summer the next stretch of cliffs teems with birdlife, as puffins, fulmars, guillemots and razorbills all vie for space on which to establish their nests. On the Stacks of Skroo and at Dronger a gannetry colony has been established and this is another excellent spot to take a break and watch the tremendous aerial activity. Climb up the slopes to reach the Trig. Pt. on top of Ward Hill (217m) which was the site of a war time radar station and a watch sight since people first came to live on Fair Isle. Enjoy superb views of the whole island and to the north the massive headlands of Fitful, Sumburgh, Noss and Bressay. Follow the cliffs round to Ler Ness where there is a prehistoric cairn and head south along another stretch of magnificent cliff scenery which includes Burrista, with its natural arch and its possible Celtic Christian monastic site dating back to the 7th century. The ruins are on an eroding promontory, access to which can only be made across a precipitous narrow track. There is speculation that it may have been an iron-age promontory fort but exploration is best

Fair Isle – Landberg Fort and North Haven.

done from some distance!

Visit the Hill Dyke. This runs alongside the ancient 'Feelie Dyke' and marks the boundary separating the northern hill land from the crofts and green fields to the south. It was originally made by the two turf dykes and then by this dry stone. The division dates back hundreds of years. At Muckle Geo of Hoini head east via the airstrip to return to The Lodge.

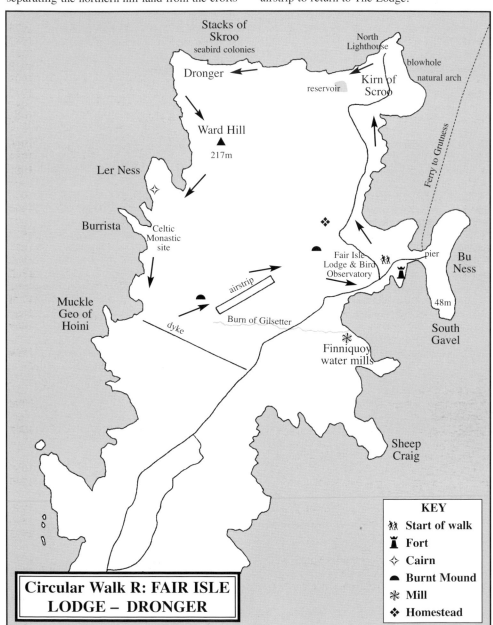

Stacks of Skroo
seabird colonies

North Lighthouse

blowhole

Dronger

natural arch

reservoir

Kirn of Scroo

Ferry to Grutness

Ward Hill
▲
217m

Ler Ness

✧

Burrista

Celtic Monastic site

airstrip

Fair Isle Lodge & Bird Observatory

pier

Bu Ness

Muckle Geo of Hoini

dyke

Burn of Gilsetter

48m

South Gavel

✳
Finniquoy water mills

Sheep Craig

KEY

🚶🚶 **Start of walk**

⚔ **Fort**

✧ **Cairn**

⬤ **Burnt Mound**

✳ **Mill**

❖ **Homestead**

Circular Walk R: FAIR ISLE
LODGE – DRONGER

110

ACKNOWLEDGEMENTS

I am indebted to the authors and editors of the following books and magazine articles and people who have helped me:

The Medieval churches and chapels of Shetland	R. G. Cant	1975
Shetland Place-names	John Stewart	1987
My Shetland	Annie Deyell	1975
The Shaping of Shetland	Ed. Val Turner	1998
Old Scatness Broch	Ed. R. A. Nicholson & S. J. Dockrill	1998
St Ninian's Isle and its Treasures 2 vols	A. Small, C. Thomas, D. Wilson	1973
The Dunrossness Story	J. W. Irvine	1987
Shetland's Northern Links	Ed. Doreen J. Waugh	1996
Songs and Sights of Shetland	Christine M. Guy	1995
Fair Isle – Archaeology of an Island Community	J. R. Hunter	1996
Shetland Shipwrecks	Shetland Sub-Aqua Club	1989
A Guide to Prehistoric Shetland	Noel Fojut	1981
A Guide to Prehistoric and Viking Shetland	Noel Fojut	1994
Drifting Alone to Norway (Betty Mouat)	Dr Mortimer Manson	1936
Jarlshof – A Walk through the Past	Historic Scotland	1000
A Guide to Shetland's Breeding Birds	Bobby Tulloch	1992
A Description of the Shetland Islands	Samuel Hibbert	1822
Shetland	Robert Cowie	1874
Guide to Shetland	Dr Mortimer Manson	1942
The Orkneys and Shetland	John R. Tudor	1883
A Brief Description of Orkney and Zetland	John Brand	1701
A Tour through the Islands of Orkney and Shetland	George Low	1774
Reminiscences of a Voyage to Shetland	Christian Ployen	1896
Art Rambles in Shetland	John Reid	1869
Shetland III ('The Inventory') The Ancient and Historic Monuments of Scotland	Royal Commission	1946
Shetland Life Magazine 1982-	Editor James R. Nicolson	
West Coast Walk	Ian J. D. Anderson	
Shetland Field Study Walks	Jill Slee Blackadder	1998
Missing Mosquito	Mike Hopkins	
The Chambered Tombs of Scotland vols 1 & 2	Audrey Shore Henshall	1965
Burnt Mound papers (including extracts from Natural Monuments record of Scotland up to 1989)	John Cruse	
Pictures from Shetland's past	Fred Irvine	1955
Iron Age Promontory Forts in the Northern Isles BAR British Series 79	Raymond Lamb	1980
Shetland – An illustrated architectural guide	Mike Finnie	1990
The Life of Sir Walter Scott	J. G. Lockhart	1896
Footsteps through Sandwick	Katrina Inkster & Marisa Harlington	1995
Coastal Settlements of the North, Scottish Archaeological Forum Vol. 5	Raymond Lamb	1973
Lerwick Town Hall – A Guide	Dr Mortimer Manson	1984
New Shetlander: Robert Leask articles	Editors L. Graham and J. Graham	
St. Ninia	John MacQueen	1961
Richard Trevithick and the Shetland Mining Company Journal of the Trevithick Society No. 17	Derek Flinn	1990

ACKNOWLEDGEMENTS

The Royal Commission on the Ancient and Historic Monuments of Scotland for the illustrations: Broch of Burland, Mail Rune Stone, Jarlshof Settlement, Broch of Levenwick, Fort Ness of Burgi, Broch of Mousa, Broch of Clickimin. Crown Copyright: Royal Commission on the Ancient and Historic Monuments of Scotland.

Thanks to Shetland Library, Chief Librarian John Hunter and his staff and to Shetland Museums Service, Museum Curator Tommy Watt and his staff particularly Vicki Gowans for help with photographs: Garth by G. W. Wilson, Quarff and Broonies' Taing by J. D. Rattar, The Shetland Cycling Club 1897 by James Prophet Isbister, Sandwick by James Manson and Tattie houses at Mail by I. M. Anonson. Copyright Shetland Museum and printed with kind permission. Papil Stone, copyright Trustees of the National Museum of Scotland. Monk's Stone, Dennis Coutts. Quendale Beast by Jack Rae, Shetland Jewellery. Dr Mortimer Manson with Yell choir by John Coutts. The book of Kells exhibition, Trinity College Library, University of Dublin. Dr Bernard Meehan, Keeper of Manuscripts and Jane Maxwell.

The following people who kindly guided me, Theo Fullerton on Burra Isle and Malcolm and Magnus Bray to the Mosquito Memorial on Royl Field, or gave me information including Sam and Joanna Christie, Betty Fullerton, Irene Bray, Jennifer Sutherland, George Mainland, Lewis and Annette Smith, Tom Angus, Brian Smith, Margaret and Tammy Irvine. Permission to print Eddie Smith's 'Da White Horse O'Hoofield' kindly given by Margaret Smith. Robert Leask, Gordon and Marjorie Williamson, Mary Ann Jamieson, Elizabeth Shearburn, John Symmons and Hugh Harrop all helped me in various ways.

All publications in this series owe their existence to the "Around the Isles" articles by "Hundiclock" published in "Sullom Voe Scene" and reporting by Nigel Martin. Grateful thanks to Janet Mullins who once again deciphered my script, tolerated my additions and amendments and prepared the book for publication.

BP Sullom Voe Terminal who sponsored photographs from the Royal Commission on the Ancient and Historical Monuments of Scotland – a donation matched from proceeds to the South Mainland Community History Group. Cartoons by Jennifer Nisbet.

Advice on accommodation is given by the Tourist Information Centre, Shetland Islands Tourism, Market Cross, Lerwick, Shetland ZE1 0LU. Telephone: 01595 693434.